What People Have to Say

"Through Siva's Grace, I experienced a miraculous healing of a debilitating disease. Siva has given me the tools to develop a new career that is personally fulfilling and financially rewarding. I had the fortune to travel to many different countries and witness Siva's infinite compassion, commitment and dedication to the material and spiritual transformation of everyone in the world. I am inspired to participate in Siva's resolve to end world hunger and poverty. My life is so rich and for the continuous blessings, I am thankful to Siva."

Arlene (Toronto, Canada)

"I recently got a gorgeous new S430 Mercedes-Benz car. When I bought it, the first thing that came to my mind was, 'Thank you Sri Siva, for changing my consciousness!!! Thank you for bringing so many good things to my life!!! Thank you for sharing your knowledge with me!!!' When I bought it, I was so excited that I was shaking and crying, because I could see how I was manifesting. From the financial standpoint, this last month has been the best in the history of our company (my husband and I own our translation and interpretation company). The company keeps on growing...We are truly manifesting what we want."

Ruth (San Diego, California, USA)

"Before meeting Sri Siva my life was in fairly decent order, but there was lots of room for improvement. I had a house and a decent job. But I was driving a beat up car with over 100,000 miles, sleeping restlessly on a junky old futon bed and dreaming about ways to end my daily work commute. Within six months of following Sri Siva's teachings I acquired a shiny new Mercedes, bought a dream bed fit for a queen, and increased my annual income by 50 percent. By the end of the year, I expect to have more than doubled that income, which gives me the breathing room to discover what I really want to do with my days. Blessings to Sri Siva and his teachings!"

Elaine (New York, New York, USA)

"I have been following Sri Siva's personal transformation program for just over a year now. Before I meet Sri Siva, I didn't have much physical energy, my financial situation was totally disorganized and lacked direction. I was shy and an overall introvert who had difficulty expressing herself and spent much of her time alone. In the last year, my hourly earnings are now DOUBLED, I've flown in private corporate helicopters with the CEO of a multi-million dollar corporation and much of my "loner" isolation is gone! And even though I see these totally miraculous results of Sri Siva's program in the physical, such as increased income, this is not what I value the most. Sri Siva's program has given me HOPE and a reason to better myself while living at this crazy time in the world where hope is often a four letter word! I feel happy and continue to be empowered by the techniques Sri Siva has revealed in his program."

Sonja (Greenwich, Connecticut, USA)

"A miracle happened: I was working on a full time job making $60,000. I received a call from a recruiter and I got a computer contract. My hourly rate increased to $85 per hour. I was impressed. Less than a year after, I got another call and now I am making $150 per hour. Everything that you really, really, really desire will happen. Sri Siva always advises us to buy good cars, especially Mercedes-Benz. He tells us that when you drive a junky car it is because you have a junky mind. Now when I drive my brand new Mercedes E320, I understand what Sri Siva means... I feel like a queen. When I drive in my Mercedes to work, it's a miraculous experience; I love to drive to work. Thanks, Sri Siva, for making a better person of my 'self' every day. Sri Siva, thanks for changing my life!"

Claudia (New York, New York, USA)

"Since I met Sri Siva (Sri Guruji), my life has changed in many ways. I couldn't think of anything better than learning the Ah meditation from the actual source. Three years later my life has evolved into an ever-changing mosaic. I am finally living life and feel that every day will be better than the day before. I have manifested a great car, a beautiful home on the lake (which really is paradise), pilgrimages to India and my work has steadily grown with profits increasing every year. I thank Siva every day."

Debra (Ontario, Canada)

"Since I have worked with Sri Siva's techniques, I have gone from making $6,000 a month to $30,000 a month. I am grateful and thankful for his influence in my life; he has shown me that miracles can happen."

Anthony (Greenwich, Connecticut, USA)

"I have been meditating for many years, but I have never had a teacher like Sri Siva."

Dennis (Albuquerque, New Mexico, USA)

"What I have gained from Sri Siva is greater self confidence, a hope for the future and a teacher to guide me. In the twelve months with him I have traveled extensively, met unique and special people, and reassessed my view of relationships, work and the way the world works. Having now received my Nadi leaf reading, my trust, faith and optimism for the road ahead has given me a vision of possibility that I have never experienced before. My life has fundamentally changed."

Dave (London, England)

"When I met Sri Siva two and a half years ago, I was in constant physical pain, overweight, working in an extremely draining profession and I felt a bottomless exhaustion. His blessings and teachings have given me a new joyful life! I am thirty pounds lighter, have incredible energy and I love life! Spiritually, I feel a deeper understanding of life and more compassion."

Ann (Bloomfield, New Jersey, USA)

"Sri Siva's ancient teachings and simple words have shaken me deeply and changed my life in many ways. On a material level, I've doubled my income, more than tripled my net worth, attained a very comfortable home, become debt free, and started enjoying the independence of working for myself. On a deeper level, his teachings have profoundly changed the way I perceive and respond to events and challenges in my life. Most importantly, his words speak directly to my inner sadness and longing for a connection to the Divine. As Sri Siva is fond of saying, 'Action is better than inaction' and, his teachings are pure action."

Vipool (Toronto, Canada)

THE ONE MINUTE GUIDE
to Prosperity and Enlightenment

Sri Siva

Vaaak Sounds • Oakmont, Pennsylvania

Visit the web site at *www.srisiva.com* for more information, products and resources.

Cover design by Joan Holman and Janelle Bilewitch
Format and Layout by Rose Jenkins

Library of Congress Cataloging-in-Publication Data

Siva, Sri.
The One Minute Guide to Prosperity and Enlightenment.

1. Spirituality   2. Prosperity   3. Self Help   4. Tamil Siddhas

Library of Congress Control Number: 2002112126

ISBN 0-9724254-0-3

Printed in Canada

Dedication

Dedicated with tears to the hungry people who end their earthly sojourn every day with parched tongues and empty stomachs.

Acknowledgements

The inspiration for this book came from the suffering of the billions that currently inhabit the earth plane. I know the Divine techniques in this book will help some people.

I want to acknowledge one person particularly in the preparation of the book. That person is Joan Holman, who made the book simple and user-friendly.

Also, Elaine Goodman deserves acknowledgement and my blessings for her valuable contributions in the preparation of the book.

Dr. Wayne Dyer made my work visible to the world. Not that I want to be visible. Visibility creates all the problems in the world. One consistent communication that came from God is, "BE INVISIBLE. DON'T YOU REALIZE THAT I AM INVISIBLE?" Visibility is Maya—the created world. I acknowledge both Wayne Dyer and Joan Holman for making an invisible man visible. Nevertheless, I will soon be invisible in a visible manner. The future will reveal the existence of my non-existence on the earth plane.

Contents

Dedication, Acknowledgements

A Message from Sri Siva

Y ou are very fortunate to be living at this time in history. We are on the threshold of earth's Golden Age, and everything is going to change for the better.

I want you to attain your optimal financial potential. I want you to get everything you desire. The techniques and tools in this book will help you create and maintain attitudes and behaviors that support and encourage a fully rounded material and spiritual consciousness. To step out of your old life and into a new life, you need Divine energy through the use of spiritual tools.

Divine help is here right now to bring you Divine awareness and create a new destiny. Ritual and practice are more important than theory. They are the keys to the manifestation of the changes you desire in your life.

I have come here to simplify things. I present simple teachings and simple techniques that are easy to practice. This book is not about philosophy. There is an expression "Philosophy never bakes bread," which is to say philosophy is not practical.

To all of you reading this book, I send blessings to empower you to live an outrageously wonderful life filled with abundance and new and expansive opportunities. My goal in this lifetime is to put money and power into the hands of spiritual people.

This book can help you manifest your dreams. The One Minute Meditation taught in this book will create miracles in your life. And there are many other techniques that take one minute or only a few minutes. You should select the techniques and rituals that best meet your needs and your schedule.

Be assured that ALL of the techniques for manifestation in this book are based upon enhancing your spirituality and cultivating your relationship with the Divine. I want to help you change your karma so you can have your heart's desire. Your karma (which is the spiritual law of cause and effect) comes from actions in your previous lifetimes.

It is not necessary to prolong your karma in the name of God. You can step right out of this karma, right now, using the techniques in this book. You can create a whole new life for yourself, a life of joy, abundance and Enlightenment.

You are reading this book because you have been led by God to know these teachings. Approach these teachings with an open mind, and just give the techniques a try.

Now, as never before in history, the floodgates of Heaven have opened to pour the Light of God into the earth plane. God is coming to earth to evolve the human race, and He is revealing His secrets to spiritual seekers.

You have a destiny. And your destiny has drawn you to The One Minute Guide to Prosperity and Enlightenment. This is my first book. It is not from "me." It is from God, and it is God's will that this book was created for you to have this information now.

The techniques in this book are for spiritual seekers of all faiths. I want to make these tools available to everyone, regardless of their faith. My desire is to help anyone who seeks Light and higher consciousness. This book is not about religion. It is about ancient spiritual practices that transcend religion. The true Universal Religion is the religion of love, and Enlightenment brings with it compassionate love for all of humanity.

I have loved everyone invariably. Love is a necessity for me. I have loved people who judged, despised, doubted and hated me. I have known many people who tell me, "We have the notoriety and money. Sri Siva hasn't even made the substantial money and notoriety that we have made."

I am here not to make substantial money and have notoriety. I am here to remove the ignorance of people. Money can't give you "samadhi" (a transcendent state of consciousness) or cure your failing kidney or liver. I am here to put money in the hands of the spiritual people who weep and cry for the hungry billions. If I have to make a choice between a beach home or the heart of a hungry soul, I will choose the latter.

Om Nama Shivaya

Sri Siva

Introduction

Yuga is the Hindu term for an age of time. These ages last thousands of years. Many, many spiritual traditions have had predictions that during the difficult and dark days of the current age, called the Kali Yuga, enlightened teachings would be made widely available and hidden knowledge would be brought into the open.

I have been tasked with bringing the wisdom of the enlightened Tamil Siddhas of India to the world and in particular to the West during this time.

As the first Tamil Siddha to travel to the West, I have been given permission to openly teach secret techniques of the Tamil Siddha enlightenment lineage which have, up to now, been held very closely. These techniques include the use of ancient formulas of Divine sounds that have immense power.

The Tamil Siddhas are native to the southern state of Tamil Nadu. They have been associated with psychokinetic powers and other paranormal phenomena including levitation, flying through the air, clairvoyance, knowledge of the future, the ability to make themselves invisible, and immortality.

The revered Indian mystic Tirumular has defined the Siddhas as those "who have experienced Divine light and Divine power from within and through Yogic Samadhi."

The term Siddha means a person with "miraculous and magical power." The Siddha supreme ideal is freedom, perfect health and immortality. The powers attained are for the purpose of benefiting others, and the true sign of an enlightened being is love and compassion.

It is my mission to open doorways to Light, normally not shared with any but the closest disciples, and to make techniques widely available through mass media and in modern technology forms (books, television, films, CDs, videos, the Internet and other modes of communication) so that all who aspire to greater freedom have an equal opportunity to experience direct blessings from the world of Enlightenment.

It is my earnest desire to instill a renewed sense of hope and faith in all seekers of Light and to share these practical Siddha techniques for peace and prosperity with all receptive, spiritually inclined persons.

This book presents several practical tools for self-improvement that can accelerate both your material progress and your path to spiritual enlightenment. My promise is a "One Minute Guide to Prosperity and Enlightenment," and indeed, there are several tools that take only one minute. There are also additional tools and techniques shared as options for those of you wishing more extensive practices. My goal is not to lead you to a life of renunciation or asceticism, or to have you shun the responsibilities of this world in favor of the spiritual world. These practices are not relevant for our contemporary civilization. Destruction of ego does not mean losing the purpose of one's life and becoming a monk or recluse. Unfortunately, this has been the interpretation in practice among most mainstream Indian traditions such as Vedanta and Buddhism.

Both the Vedantians and the Buddhists leave the world and their responsibilities in favor of the other world. True, they kill their ego, but only through denial of a phenomenal existence. It's not a desirable model. In fact, this perception has created extreme poverty consciousness in India, and poverty consciousness among many sincere spiritual seekers worldwide.

There are very important messages in the Bible that come through the life of Jesus. People told Jesus that they would believe him if he could manifest bread for them from heaven just as Moses did. Jesus said that he could do even better and give them eternal life. People couldn't have cared less, and I don't blame them. At the end of the day what matters is that you have bread on your table. Jesus then manifested food for 5,000 people.

When I go around the world giving talks, people ask me if I can manifest a trinket for them like Sai Baba does. I tell them, "No, I can't do it. However, I can manifest a Mercedes-Benz for you, although you may have bad credit and no money for a down payment." I am a spiritual teacher, and a realist, and I can help you spiritually and practically. Both methods are important. Spiritually, I want you to believe that I can help you. How can I help you if you don't believe? You may ask me, "What if I don't have faith?" And I say that you must cultivate faith. It is a positive quality. There are exercises in this book that will help to create faith.

From the several tools and techniques presented in this book, you should select two or three to try out in your own life. The tools are not ordinary human tools. Human devices take too long to manifest. This book contains Divine devices that will restructure your reality. As you use these tools, you must be very clear about your goals and have the resolve to achieve these goals. People do not manifest because they do not remember what they want to manifest. Always stay conscious and fully focused on what you want to manifest. As a spiritual teacher, my goal is to bring you both Prosperity and Enlightenment. Money will not give you Enlightenment, but it will give you a sense of safety and security to pursue a meditational practice.

This book is dedicated to those spiritual seekers who wish to embrace and embody the Light and Love and Abundance of the Divine, not only in Heaven, but also on earth.

⤳

Chapter 1

The Age of Miracles

Good things are going to happen.

According to Vedic astrology, the Sun, Moon, Mars, Mercury, Saturn, Venus and Rahu (in Western astrology Rahu is the north Node of the Moon) moved into Taurus on May 14, 2002. This was potentially the most dangerous combination for the welfare of the planet. Due to the grace of God, this danger was averted. Hereafter, there will not be a major apocalypse. Shiva wants to give an opportunity for people to turn to God.

(Note: In the Hindu religion, God or the Supreme Being is conceived as having several aspects. Lord Shiva represents an aspect of God involved in the cyclic process of creation, preservation, dissolution and recreation of the Universe. He is generally considered the third member of the Hindu Trinity, the other two being Lord Brahma and Lord Vishnu.)

Every religious tradition has prophecies that the End of Times is coming. Is there any truth to it? Yes, there is. It is indeed the apocalyptic time. The Bible says in the Revelation that at the End of Times there will be trouble for Israel. And, God and Jesus will come to rescue it. Most importantly, God is going to stay on the earth plane along with human beings, and rule like a king.

The End of Times
The End of Times will be a time for miracles in the sky. People will be able to see Jesus and the angels in the sky. It is not easy for the human mind to

think that this is all real. The Apostle Paul says that the corrupt physical body will change into a pure body in order to receive the kingdom. Other religions have their own view of the End of Times. The Buddhists are expecting the Maitreya (a future Buddha), the Hindus are waiting for the Kalki avatar, and the Native Americans are looking for the White Buffalo. One truth of all these prophecies is, "Yes, the wonderful times are coming soon."

The Age of Miracles Arrived June 14, 2002

I want to add my own prophecy here. The Age of Miracles (also known as the Age of Truth) officially dawned on June 14, 2002. After June 14th the world passed through an unexpected turn of destiny. Destiny had it that there was going to be natural calamities and nuclear war destroying large scales of people. All over the globe. But, God intervened and changed the rules. The developments in the Middle East took an unexpected turn resulting in the humbling of Arafat followed by the mysterious silence of the Arab world over this matter. The almost inevitable war between India and Pakistan came to an end.

Human Consciousness Will Change

The most important change will be taking place within our minds and the way we think. Human consciousness itself will change and be filled with love and joy. Doubt, jealousy, anger, hatred, vengeance, and deceit will be reduced to a minimum. There won't be any walls between countries. Anyone will go anywhere without passports or visas. No one will be left behind without food, clothing, and housing. The Age of Miracles will have two major impacts. It will make the impure people pure, and it will turn the pure people into angels, meaning some people will attain light bodies through God's grace.

God Is Light, God Is Love

I will be teaching many special techniques during the Age of Miracles. And I want you to rest assured that the Age of Miracles has truly arrived. You may ask, "Who is going to come? Jesus, Maitreya, Kalki or the White Buffalo?" I want you to understand God has no name or form. Everyone understands within his or her parameter. In my opinion God is Light, God is Love. He or She or the androgyne (I like the androgyne better!!) will help everyone to open his or her third eye, an energy center located between the eyebrows that is the seat of intuition and awareness.

Most Auspicious Time in the History of the Universe

We are living in the most auspicious time in the history of the Universe. At this time, right now, tremendous spiritual energy is available for you to change your life into the life of your dreams. The great Divine Being Lord Shiva is going to electrify the planet and make it luminous. Lord Shiva has existed prior to consciousness and creation. From time to time he has revealed himself indirectly through his saints, devotees, and in the dream plane of some individuals, and he is revealing much at this time about the unprecedented opportunity for mankind to advance its spiritual evolution faster and farther than ever before in history.

The Time Is Perfect for Accelerated Spiritual Practices

The energy conditions in the world at this time are perfect for the accelerated, fast working spiritual practices that I am teaching. Normally, this advancement in spiritual evolution would require lifetimes of rigorous, devoted practice. However, right now, the Divine is pouring light into our hearts and minds to rebuild a higher, happier consciousness and bring in the promised new Golden Age. I am maximizing this Divine outpouring by providing previously secret practices specifically designed to accelerate spiritual development, with the permission from my tradition to share this knowledge openly for the first time, because the time is right.

Chapter 2

Putting Money into the Hands of the Spiritual People

*To run away from the world
is to run away from God.*

W
e are living on the threshold of a New Age in which there will be a paradigm shift. I predict that within just a few years, money and power are going to be in the hands of the spiritual community.

Spiritual People Shy Away from Money

In general, spiritual people shy away from money. This is an historic truth. Examine the following statement from the Bible, "It is easier for a camel to pass through the eye of a needle than for a rich man to enter the kingdom of God." You go to church/temple/mosque and all of a sudden you become very grave. You seem to think that God might love long faces, because your concept of God is that He is a killjoy and a peeping Tom. It is time that spiritual people change their negative attitude towards money and material life.

I Am Committed to Putting Money and Power into the Hands of Spiritual People

Currently, most of the money is in the hands of people who are totally unconscious. Most rich people are self-centered, egocentric and want to grow richer and richer at any cost. They don't even realize that they have more money than they could possibly spend in this lifetime. They have no sympathy for the three billion human beings who go to bed hungry. There is no willingness to share their wealth. Conversely, the poor and the spiritual people want to share whatever they have with those who are in need. Unfortunately, because these people don't have money, their sympathy has very little impact.

Spiritual People Need to Become More Active, Not Otherworldly

Fundamentally, spiritual people should come out of the closet and become more active. It is important for them to understand that if you meditate for longer hours and spend a lot of time reflecting on God, over a period of time you will become otherworldly. In some cases, it may even create depression and a lack of interest in being active.

Spiritual People Must Remain Grounded

It is important that all spiritual people do something to remain grounded. You can practice a martial art or some other form of physical exercise that will keep you alert.

Some Tips to Radically Change Your Mind

Perhaps you have been a monk or ascetic for many lifetimes. In those lifetimes, your priority had only been God. You rejected relationships, worldly pleasures, politics, and other activities in favor of a reclusive and ascetic life. These strong memories from past lives should be erased. I have dedicated a meditation for this problem that you will find in this book. It is called "The Karma-Busting Mantra."

The World Is the Creation of God

It is important to get rid of the concepts that this world is an illusion and that it is important to only focus attention on God rather than the world. You must realize that the world with all its complexity and silliness is still the creation of God. When you are having a good meal, enjoying beautiful music, communing with Nature, know that you are connecting with God. To run away from the world is to run away from God.

Power and Money Must Change Hands

I am currently putting out a lot of my energy to give spiritual people the tools they need to become prosperous. The world will not see any substantial progress unless money and power change hands. From time immemorial, money has always remained in the hands of the wrong people. No more can we allow this to happen. Already the world has suffered. Let us bring all the spiritual people together and work towards this goal.

During the last few years, Wayne Dyer and Deepak Chopra have done important work in this area. I congratulate both of them for their extraordinary work. I gave a secret meditation for manifestation particularly to Wayne Dyer called the Ah meditation, which he presents in his book *Manifest Your Destiny*, and which I discuss in this book. The Ah mantra is being practiced all over the world and I have heard many people speak about their success with it.

Global Meditation Group

Let us bring all the spiritual people together and work towards the goal of putting the money and power in the hands of the spiritual people. It is my desire to start a global meditation group that will meet at specific times of the day to bring in the Golden Age. The group will use the Internet to facilitate this change of power. Visit my web site at *www.srisiva.com* to check on the status of this program.

Chapter 3

Karma and Destiny

Karma is one's destiny.
There is a way out of your karma.

Y ou have created misery through the power of your past actions and thoughts, which is your karma. Karma is the spiritual law of cause and effect. Through good acts you create good karma, and through bad acts you create bad karma. For instance, if you have done good actions in your past lives, this lifetime will bring a life of luxury, good health and happiness. Conversely, bad actions from past lives will create problems, suffering and poverty in this lifetime.

The Nature of Karma

The literal meaning of karma is action. Action in this case needs to be defined not only as an impulse at the physical level, but also an impulse at a subtle or psychological level. Hence, thinking is action.

Thoughts Create Karma

Everything that you think creates vibrations and leaves impressions. The Buddha said that one's whole life consists of one's thoughts. This is the best definition of karma I have ever found. You caused the life that you are now living. You may not like the reality that you have created, but at the moment you created it you thought that this was the best that could be accomplished. That's why you created it. When did you create it? You created it in a number of previous births. The desire to create this reality was so intense that you ended up creating it. Nobody was responsible but you.

Why did you do this? You did not know any better at the time you created it.

Your Soul Remembers Karma

How is karma carried from one life to another? How can the thoughts from one lifetime be remembered in the next? Your soul remembers these thoughts and seeks to be born in an environment where these thoughts can be realized. Your soul is just a collection of electrical energy. Through breath awareness, you can access your soul; you can see and understand your future possibilities. Once you recognize the things that are waiting to happen, you can diffuse a lot of desires that are not life supporting, which you have created out of ignorance.

There Is a Way Out of Karma

You may ask, "Is there a way out of my misery or do I have to suffer to my death? If that is what karma means, do I have any hope?" Yes, you do. But it is difficult to make changes in this area. Why is it difficult? Because you are fighting against material reality.

Two Kinds of Reality: Spiritual and Material

Reality is of two kinds. One is a spiritual reality, and another is a material reality. Let me give you an example. There is ice, snow, water, steam—all of which are H_2O. They are different stages of H_2O at different temperatures. When H_2O becomes ice, it acquires maximum physicality.

Material Reality Is Difficult to Change

It is very difficult to change the structure of the ice because it has become like a stone, very hard. But when it is snow, it is easy to change. When it is steam, it is easier to change. But now, at this phase, we are living a material life that is comparable to the ice. That's why it is difficult to change.

Change Requires Spiritual Energy

But, remember, I am not saying that it is impossible to change. It is possible to change, but it requires energy to wake up and diffuse your karma. You can diffuse materiality, the material elements that are going to come that you created in your past births.

How to Change Your Destiny

How can you change or diffuse this karma you have created and thus change your destiny? In order to understand how to diffuse karma, you must understand what life is and how karma is related to life. You can challenge karma this very moment by making a very strong decision. The Buddha had a very strong karma to become a king, but he had no interest in playing this part. To be a ruler and wield great power might be of interest to others, but the Buddha wanted no part in this kind of drama. How did the Buddha challenge this karma? He made a decision to quit that life, and he took nothing from that life with him. Kingdom, wife, child, even food or clothing, nothing mattered to him but the search for consciousness. In this way, the Buddha challenged his karma.

You change your destiny by making a decision to change your life and by becoming alert. All you need to do to diffuse your karma is to dispel the spell. You are under a spell. You are like a robot. You are asleep although you say you are in a waking state. You have to become alert to the core. You have to create more energy to diffuse the karma.

With Alertness, You Challenge Your Karma

When you become alert, you begin to challenge reality, challenge karma. When you challenge karma, you are not going to accept things as they are. Every minute you are going to be conscious. At no time are you going to be unconscious. If you are unconscious, you are allowing things to happen. You are causing the karma to manifest. The moment you become alert, you challenge karma. So the way to diffuse karma is to become alert and not allow the robot to continue in the way it is continuing.

Live Life with Consciousness

It requires a tremendous amount of spiritual energy to do things better. You are not going to live life the way you have lived so far. The way you have lived so far is to just live life without consciousness. We love to forget ourselves. We have no consciousness to realize that we are breathing. That's why the Buddha said that, at least for an hour, you should become conscious of your breathing. And he said that while you are doing this exercise, you have to be so conscious that you should not even miss one breath. Because the breath and the mind are related processes. Yet even for five minutes, you cannot put your mind on the breath. If you have successfully become aware of your breath for an hour, that will change your life entirely because by that time you will have created enough energy, enough alertness, to diffuse karma.

Attention Diffuses Karma

Attention will diffuse karma. If you are attentive, things cannot get over-looked. You can stop things by virtue of your own attention. You don't have much attention now. You just allow things to happen. So with attention, you can stop things. This is the law of Nature. Attention means care. Attention and care are synonymous. If you bring more attention, you bring more care. You don't care now. Mike Tyson has great muscles that you and I don't have. Why? Did he care for his muscles? He did. Did you care for your muscles? No. And how did he care for them? His whole life was his muscles. So what you need is care, more attention. When you bring more attention, then you become more alert. Then karma will stop.

Karma stops because you are waking up to a different dimension of existence where you are able to see the karma coming forth, and then the attention burns the karma. This is how you avoid the dangers that are yet to come.

The Need to Meditate

Patanjali, the enlightened Indian yogi who collected the *Yoga Sutras*, stated why people need to meditate. You have to meditate because you have to avoid the danger that has not yet come. You have created enough dangers for several lifetimes. They are unfolding. This lifetime is not enough to live those events, so you are going to create other lives to enjoy it or suffer it. So what you have to do is just meditate more.

What Is Meditation

To meditate means to think, to think deeply. In Sanskrit, the word for meditation means thinking deeply. So meditation doesn't really mean keeping your eyes closed. Anything that you deeply, deeply think is meditation. Even people who are constantly thinking about something they want to manifest are in meditation.

By Meditating You Create More Awareness

The Buddha sat under the bodhi tree before his enlightenment, and he began to re-live all the karma that he had to pass through, and he emptied it. Then, there was no more karma to emerge. That is why he said that total reality is emptiness. There is nothing out there and, in that emptiness, you are full. Emptiness is not a negative quality. Emptiness is unlimited life in which you are not defined. You are infinite. And that, Buddha said, is the

15

true nature of every human being, to live without karma. That state is produced by awareness.

The Tamil Siddha Tradition

The Tamil Siddha tradition believes in changing life both materially and spiritually. You have to challenge your material reality and change it not for the next life, but right now for this life itself.

To Change Your Destiny,
Change the Sounds in Your Consciousness

The mind is a bunch of sounds. This is the model of the Siddhas. And what did they mean by the statement that your mind is a bunch of sounds? Your mind is made up of language. Ninety percent of your mind is language. If you pull out language from the mind, the mind would not exist. Then, what is language? Language is sound—sound and meaning put together. Now, what is sound? Sound is just a bunch of vowels and consonants. If you understand vowels and consonants, you have understood most of your mind. So, if you want to change your mind, change the sounds in your consciousness. Your mind has a sound pattern. Your unconscious has a sound pattern. Change these patterns and you will find yourself manifesting the life of your dreams. By using the mantras presented in this book, you can change your destiny by changing the sounds of your consciousness. Mantra, combined with intention and attention, will create miracles in your life. I could probably write a PhD dissertation on this topic, but it is not necessary now. Ten years ago I would have done it. I am now precise and into Timelessness.

Chapter 4

Take Control of Your Thoughts

Everything that happens in your life depends
upon how you spend your thought energy.

You are your thoughts.

Everything that happens in your life depends upon how you spend your thought energy. Everything starts with your thinking process. So you should constantly be absorbed in looking at what you are thinking. Whatever you think becomes a reality in the invisible space-time complex of your soul, and then it manifests after an appropriate lapse of time. Everything is created by your mind. So you have to become very, very responsible in handling your mind, because whatever you think is going to become a reality. Your life is a result of your own thoughts in past lives. You have to become very, very careful about what you think, because what you think is going to manifest as reality.

Observe Your Thoughts

If you begin to observe your thoughts, you will find that all the thoughts that you have, or ninety-nine percent of them, are devoted to this world:

▲ How can I survive in this world?
▲ What are my relationships with others?
▲ What are my job situations?
▲ What about my health?

All these questions are worldly thoughts. And these are the thoughts that occupy you all the time. So, once you observe these thoughts, worldly thoughts, then you have a choice to go with them or to regulate them. And those people who want to regulate these thoughts will eventually, at some point, begin to understand the need to get liberated from the thought process. This is your first step. It is important to realize that it is very difficult to stay away from your worldly thoughts. It is because you live in this material plane, which makes constant demands on you to stay focused on the thoughts about day-to-day survival.

The Demands of the Material Plane

You are also under constraints to act in accordance with your karma, which brings you a set of thoughts with it. These are thoughts that you decided to think in this lifetime. Then there is Maya (or illusion), which always keeps you engaged.

So, the bottom line is you acknowledge that it is difficult to not think thoughts about this world, and that these thoughts about this world are almost an involuntary process. It goes on even without asking your permission to think or not to think. It seems to be an autonomous process. But it is not so. The moment you begin to evaluate your own thinking process, you will understand that you really do have a choice to either think worldly thoughts or go to the spiritual plane and think thoughts about Enlightenment and higher states of consciousness.

Carefully Choose Your Thoughts

There are two things you need to do. One is to look at this overwhelming experience of processing worldly thoughts. Second is to look at the thoughts about the other world and Enlightenment. You may want to begin dealing with the worldly thoughts. How do we deal with the worldly thoughts? It is not a good idea to get rid of them. You may want to do that. But you cannot. At best you can do one thing. And that is to choose the worldly thoughts you want to think and then to stick with them.

Focus Thoughts on What You Want

I want to give you some guidelines. You wake up in the morning and there are a number of obligations for that day and you need to think about them. However, you should also come up with a set of thoughts that you want to think about on a daily basis, thoughts that are very productive. Of course, you need to be thinking on a regular basis about your finances and other important considerations, but do so with positive thoughts and not fear and negativity. There are some options. You have a job and your job gives you a certain amount of money. In most cases, the money is not enough. You need to do something to change the situation. How do you do that? You must think of a sum of money, which is more than you are now making. And that will give you a new consciousness. You may not find a way to make that money right away. You may not even know how that money is going to come to you.

Bring in Divine Energy

Here are some Divine principles to help bring more money to you. As your goal, you put out a reasonable amount of money. You should not be greedy, but select an amount that can give you a reasonably good life so that you do not have to work until the end of your life on this earth plane. Once you have that amount in your mind, pray to God. Bring in the Divine energy. The Divine will help you manifest it. You do not have to really stretch your mind to figure out the means. The Divine will give you the means and the end down the road. All that you need to do is to consistently think it as a contemplation and then make the prayer periodically. You may want to do it at least twice a day where you can spend at least 15 to 20 minutes on this thought and then you can periodically remember the thought, too. Once you do this, you will find that you are manifesting this situation. This is a way to take control of your worldly thoughts. Similarly, you have to entertain thoughts about your health and physical fitness. That is very, very important. You may want to regulate the food that you are eating and perform a little bit of exercise that you require to keep your body in good shape.

Thoughts Are Your Guests

Treat your thoughts as your house guests. They check in and check out of your home. You are the host. No thought can remain within the system forever. Become alert. The thought will fall away like a dead leaf from a tree. The moment you become aware and tell yourself, "This thought is trying to cheat me and make me unhappy, I dismiss it," the thought will fall away. Thought control is an essential part of manifesting a life of Prosperity and Enlightenment.

Chapter 5

Keys for Manifestation

*Learn to substitute the
positive dream for the negative dream.*

If you can dream it, you can have it.

The secret of manifestation is to simply hold the thought of manifestation without interruption from other thoughts. The problem is that it is impossible for most people to hold onto the same thought for an extended period of time. But, this is what the yogis do. They pick up a thought and meditate on it for years. To make the process work and to be without external distractions, they go to the Himalayas. The tools in this book will help you become aware of your thoughts and focus your thoughts.

Manifestation Is Dreaming

Manifestation is just dreaming. There is a very close relationship between getting rich in a dream and getting rich in reality. Both are dreams. You think that only the dream at night is unreal. But the reality you experience in the waking state is also a dream. When you realize that, you are enlightened. Now, what you might want to consider is how to dream in the waking state reality.

How, you say, can you dream a house or a relationship or a job or whatever you want into your reality? Carlos Castaneda talks about his master who taught him the art of dreaming. His master tells him, "Just start dreaming and dreaming and dreaming to understand a great deal of the secret of the relationship between matter and spirit."

All that you need to do is to live in this dream state, even while you are awake. How? Just remember the dream. You make your cells remember that you are living the dream. Or say you are sitting at a dirty table eating breakfast. You may as well want a nicer table. And then you see a servant bringing your breakfast. You look up and around and you see a magnificent French crystal chandelier on the ceiling and paintings of famous contemporary artists all over the walls. While you eat, you imagine yourself looking out the window and seeing one of your gardeners working on the grounds. So your dream of a mansion begins to take on form. And you begin to live your dream. Learn to substitute the positive dream for the negative dream. This is very important.

Fantasy and Reality Are Not Very Different

The most important thing that the mind has to understand is that fantasy and reality are not very different. When your fantasies gain enough strength to become reality within your own consciousness, there will be no distinction between fantasy and reality. Fantasy is phenomenon that is not yet realized. Reality is a realized fantasy. So you have to make every fantasy of yours become real.

Lack of Forceful Thoughts Leads to Lack of Manifestation

If things do not happen, it is because your thoughts of manifestation lack force. You have to create forceful thoughts that stay longer in your consciousness. Continually think forceful thoughts. Think forceful thoughts over and over and over again for long periods of time. Then those thoughts will become very powerful, and the manifestation will occur sooner.

Affirmations

Use affirmations for the things that you desire to manifest in your life.

▲ I want the next unconditional moment to be full of creativity.
▲ I want the next unconditional moment to be full of creativity.
▲ I want in the next hour to realize my manifestations.
▲ I want in the next hour to realize my manifestations.
▲ I want my abundance to come to me without my thinking about it.
▲ I want my abundance to come to me without my thinking about it.

Stop Limited Thinking

For manifestation to occur, you must stop your limited thinking. I give you manifestation tools in this book. However, you have to be committed to authentic desires for these tools to work. Don't put a cap or limitation on your imagination. Any cap you put on your imagination is arbitrary and comes from your own negativity. This negativity you may have picked up through your parents, grandparents, religious conditioning or other sources. So, the first step that you have to do is to remove your limited thinking. Once you have broken the limitation on your imagination, you can go and build a new reality.

Giving the Divine Forces an Opportunity to Work in Your Life

When you remove your misconceptions, you give the Divine forces an opportunity to work. When you say, "I have no money," or other negative statements, you freeze reality. Make provision for things to happen in the NOW. Time is an illusion. Don't stop the blessings. They are already available in the NOW. You block the blessings through your own perception. You must conceive of outrageous outcomes. You can have everything in the NOW provided you make a commitment to a different kind of thinking. This is accomplished through the science of spirituality. Spirit is unlimited. It is only matter that is limited. With spirit everything is possible. We have to bring spirituality back into our lives. Being spiritual means being positive, being unlimited, being joyous forever and ever.

Get Out of the "Life Is Suffering" Mindset

Most people have been taught that life is suffering. This is all wrong thinking, wrong teaching. We have to get back to our own original unlimited Self, which is pure unending joy. This will be part of our consciousness in the Age of Miracles. Currently, many people have become specialists in impossibilities. "Forget it, I can't afford it right now. I can't even afford a two-bedroom apartment. How do you think I can buy a house?" The moment you have said this to yourself you will never be able to buy a house, because you are being negative. Somewhere, something has gone deeply wrong within us if we cannot even wish good things for ourselves.

Desire Is Necessary for Manifestation

We cannot wish that we could have a beach house. Why not? Because the logic kicks in, "No, no, there is no money." Money is not needed. What is needed is just the pure desire to have a beautiful beach house. Once the desire is there, then you can manifest it. This is the bottom line. How can you get that desire into your consciousness? That is the key issue. There are spiritual techniques in this book that will change the very core of your consciousness so that you will be able to alter your negativity. Change your life through your own spirituality. Use spiritual principles to enhance your practical life on this earth plane.

Whatever You Put in Your Consciousness Will Manifest

Consciousness is everything. Once you have the consciousness, then you can change anything. Whatever you put in your consciousness will manifest. If you put a junky car in your consciousness, a junky apartment in your consciousness, these will manifest for you. Don't blame God; don't blame your destiny; don't blame your lack of education. Don't blame anyone or anything. If you have to blame someone, blame yourself.

Blaming Other People Is a Cop-Out

To blame someone else is a cop-out. There is nobody else to blame but you. You are the creator of all these dramas. You can create a good drama or a bad drama, but you have to take responsibility for whatever you create. There is never a period in your life that you are a victim. You are never a victim. You can just walk out and say, "Goodbye, I can't take this misery any more. I have just committed myself to happiness, to unending happiness." Then you realize it is in your life. It is very important to understand how powerful you are. Rather than complain to others about being a victim to this situation, realize that you are not a victim. You are the solution, the opportunity.

Make Provision for Things to Happen Immediately

There was a woman I met in Pasadena, California, many years ago. She came to me and said, "Sri Siva, I want to buy a house next year." I said, "Why do you want to buy it next year?" She said, "It is because of practical concerns." She explained that she had just gotten a job and needed to save up money for a down payment.

In her mind, by next year she would have money saved up to be able to buy a house. However, this woman could have decided to buy a house even before one year was up. She was not giving opportunity to other forces beyond her control to work in her favor. Think about this. You may lose

23

your job within a year. Then you may not be able to buy the house at all. I am not saying that you should not plan. Everyone should plan. But you should also make provision for things to happen momentarily because time is an illusion. You should plan to have it NOW. When you decide not to buy a house sooner, you are not allowing things to happen in the NOW. You are stopping the timeless blessings. Unfortunately, the mind wants to proceed in logical sequences. It does not want to go to the end result right at the beginning.

I have come here to this earth plane in order to promote outrageous thinking. I have come here to give you thinking outside of time. I have come here to tell you how you can have everything in an hour, provided you make a commitment to a different kind of thinking.

Waiting Is a Waste of Time

Waiting is a waste of time. Just get this idea into your consciousness. We don't want to wait. We want it right now. The moment you make the decision, "I want it now," you will begin creating what you ask for.

Manifestation in the NOW

In God's consciousness the thought and its object exist in blissful union. God switches back and forth between thought and object with utmost ease. God manifests things as soon as the thought comes into His mind. This is called manifestation in the NOW. It is a simple and joyful process. For human beings, manifestation of desired objects is a complex process, which does not happen in the NOW. We need to create an action and wait until it is complete to manifest things. For instance, if we need money we first need to create a job or business to generate income, or we have to borrow from someone. However, the requirement of an action to manifest material reality appears to be redundant.

Who Is God?

Who is God? Where does God live? How can we learn this technique? God lives within you as the non-ego consciousness, without any identity whatsoever. We can learn God's consciousness if we can get rid of our ego-self. We need innocence and purity of heart. We need to be utterly simple and honest. With that, manifestation becomes easy.

The NOW of God

Human beings are unable to conceive of the NOW of God, which is also the Eternal Now. This is because human consciousness believes and lives in linear reality—a past, present and future that are spread out in a line on the earth plane in a time-space continuum.

We love the drama of life, which consists of love and longing, and success and failure. The Truth about Time, however, is that everything is in the NOW. You don't need to wait until the future to manifest things—you can manifest right NOW. Nevertheless, you don't want to manifest NOW because you are afraid and unsure of many things.

Why You Do Not Manifest NOW

This checklist will help you to identify the problems:

▲ Afraid of success because of its newness and unfamiliarity
▲ Satisfied with the current state of affairs and do not want to venture into something new
▲ Afraid of hurting others
▲ Skeptical of success
▲ Lazy and lack motivation
▲ Lack the resources
▲ Lack the qualifications

Overcoming Delays to Your Manifestation

You might want to go over and over the checklist to identify your problems. Maybe none of these categories describe your situation very well. This will, however, help you look at yourself more closely. Write down what you think are the problems that delay manifestation for you. Sincerely pray to have these problems dissolved. Praying like that is like putting your request into a microwave to get resolved faster. Ask yourself the question every hour or two during the day, "Why am I not manifesting NOW?" Keep a journal and review it on a weekly basis.

The Importance of Belief in God

There are people who attend my lectures, purchase my CDs and try the mantras I teach, and then they ask why things are still not working. Why is God not responding to you? It is because you don't believe in God. You may say to yourself that you believe in God. But the truth is, you believe only in your ego and in the world. You either think about yourself, which is your ego-self, or about the world. God has not been the priority in this Dark Age. That's why there is so much suffering and agony.

Your Consciousness Is Defined by the People around You

If you are around people who give out affluent, healthy, positive vibrations, then your mind will keep company with those thoughts. On the other hand, if you are with people who produce skeptical, negative thoughts, then you will fall victim to these thought processes. It is very important to be around people who are positive and harmonious.

For Manifestation, Nothing Is Greater than God's Name

Jesus said frequently, "Believe in me, and my name can do everything for you." Let us be honest. How many people really believe in the name of Jesus and its ability to accomplish things for them? You may say, "I have prayed in Jesus' name many times, but nothing has happened."

All that I can tell you is that there is nothing greater than God's name. But you must believe whole-heartedly and be emotionally able to relate to the Divine name that you call on for help.

For instance, if you are a devout Christian, you may not be able to call on Allah, Buddha or Shiva. Yet, I have been able to perform miracles in the lives of individuals of many different faiths who trusted me totally. Then there are others who claim that they are following me, but they are only following themselves. Jesus said, "Love me," but how many people really do love Jesus?

Spiritual Surrender Is the Key to Power and Manifestation

Another question many people ask me is, "Isn't surrender becoming powerless?" To be honest, this is a question that all spiritual aspirants ask at some point. The answer is, "No." In fact, true spiritual surrender is a powerful state. What you surrender is your limited ego to the Higher Self or God. This allows for higher intelligence to guide your life. When you give away your ego, you are giving away something that doesn't really belong to you.

↝

Chapter 6

The Indispensable Mantra—Om Nama Shivaya

(Pronounced: Om Nah-mah Shee-vah-yah)

> *The most important mantra*
> *is OM NA MA SHI VA YA.*

The most important mantra in this book is Om Nama Shivaya. If you do nothing else suggested in this book, you should chant this mantra every day. Om Nama Shivaya will open new ways to make money, be healthy, and improve your life. It will give you Divine Intelligence to know what to do to manifest your desires. It will do a world of good beyond belief. It will help you to be in the right place at the right time doing the right thing. It harmonizes you with all the elemental energies.

▲ Om is God.
▲ God is Om.
▲ Om is the primordial sound from which everything emanated.
▲ Om is consciousness.
▲ Om is Life.

The Significance of Om Nama Shivaya

The purpose of Om Nama Shivaya is very meaningful. The domain of Om is incomprehensible to the human mind. Om is the realm of all possibilities. Om is Light. Om is Arul, the Divine Intelligence. When you have enough Grace, Om will manifest as Divine Light just in front of you and will envelop you. This Light of Om will dissolve your ignorance. Different Enlightened Beings belonging to different religions have encountered the

Om Light prior to their Enlightenment. The Om Light is Allah, Shiva, Yaweh, the Tao, and Nirvana.

Nama represents lower worldly realities like earth and water and the karmic and egocentric life. When saying Nama, visualize a home, a nicer car, a healthy body. For wealth do not concentrate on just money as a concept, but precise images. Be focused on what you need — the actual things you need. For example, you can visualize physical money as loads of bills stacked on tables, or baskets of gold coins, or a wallet filled with thousand dollars bills.

Shivaya represents higher life and Shivaya gives the awareness of the Divine existence, which is the right of every human soul. When saying Shiva (pronounced shee-va), know that Shi is energy, Enlightenment, wisdom, all knowingness. Va is material energy. You are a material being. Ya is space energy. When chanting this part of the mantra, remember that the portion with the sound Shiva will bring a tremendous amount of energy. Never forget the sound Shiva. This is the greatest mantra. Cultivate the habit of the sound Shiva in your life.

The Effect of Chanting Om Nama Shivaya

The chanting of Om Nama Shivaya does the following. Om cleans up the consciousness. Nama awakens the lower realities necessary for earthly existence. Shivaya helps you to be grounded in awareness of the Divine. One should chant Om Nama Shivaya with this full understanding.

How to Chant Om Nama Shivaya

Due to the enduring power of this mantra, there are literally thousands of ways to chant it. I recommend two easy ways to quickly benefit from this mantra's extraordinary power. The first method is an even, steady-paced chant of Om Nama Shivaya done 108 times each day, ideally using Shiva-Shakti mala beads (available for purchase through Vaaak Sounds). This actually only takes a few minutes. The second method is the One Minute Meditation, which is discussed in the next chapter. Remember that consistency, combined with faith, is what brings results. Chanting Om Nama Shivaya is great to do throughout the day to keep your mind focused on higher thoughts and energies. You can even do the chants while performing other tasks. Having a watch that beeps each hour to remind you to say the chant (and focus on your manifestation goals) is one good approach. Be creative with how you remind yourself throughout the day.

Put Shiva in Your Consciousness

Let the sound of Shiva be running in your consciousness side by side with whatever you are doing. This will bring energy to manifest whatever you want. Live your life as though you have already manifested your desires. Don't give energy to fear and doubt. Always stay in a positive mode and with the sound Shiva.

≫

Chapter 7

The One Minute Meditation

One Minute to Prosperity and Enlightenment.

A s I have stated, the most important mantra in this book is OM NA MA SHI VA YA (Om Nama Shivaya). Even if you don't use any other techniques from the book, do use this mantra. It is a Divine tool that can not only improve every aspect of your life, but also improve conditions on the entire planet.

There is a powerful meditation you can do using the mantra Om Nama Shivaya. The One Minute Meditation, when practiced even just once a day, will create positive change in your life. For greater power, you can do it twice a day, from one to five times each session (one to five minutes). You can do the One Minute Meditation with your eyes open or closed. It can be done silently, out loud for greater focus, or both.

To quickly and easily get started using the One Minute Meditation, follow the explanation below. For easier understanding, this explanation breaks the chant into two units – Om and Nama Shivaya. When you do the chant, combine both units into a single one-minute cycle (35 seconds for Om, 25 seconds for Nama Shivaya).

Practice Om in the Following Way

Om is formed of three sounds: Ah, Oo, Ma. Count the time with the fingers of the right hand. Each finger will bow down and contact the right thumb. Counting five fingers is five seconds, ten seconds is two rounds of counting. At the level of human existence, Ah creates the waking state of human consciousness, Oo, the dream state, and Ma, the sleep state.

Meditate on Ah for 10 seconds at the root chakra located at the base of your spine. (Chakras are energy centers located at various places in the body). Keep repeating this sound mentally. This will attract all worldly things to you.

Meditate on Oo at the heart center for 10 seconds. This will give you Divine Intelligence and influence your dreaming.

Meditate on Ma at the throat chakra (located at the throat center) for 5 seconds. Ma will create awareness of Maya (illusion). It will create earthly consciousness and provide rest to the system. We sleep one third of our lives, so that is why Ma is for a shorter duration, so you do not become too sleepy.

Meditate on Om at the third eye chakra (located at the brow) for 10 seconds.

Om Nama Shivaya

Nama Shivaya has two units. NA MA is to be chanted at the root chakra and the navel chakra respectively. Nama represents lower worldly realities like earth and water and the karmic and egocentric life. Shivaya is the second unit. It represents higher life. SHI VA YA has to be chanted at the heart, throat and two eyes respectively. Shivaya gives the awareness of the Divine existence, which is the right of every human soul.

- ▲ NA - root center, earth energy - 5 seconds
- ▲ MA - navel center, water energy - 5 seconds
- ▲ SHI - heart center, fire energy - 5 seconds
- ▲ VA - throat and nostrils, wind/air energy - 5 seconds
- ▲ YA - two eyes, two brains, third eye, space energy - 5 seconds

The total time for one round is one minute. This One Minute Meditation can be practiced in a variety of ways. If you desire, you can stay at different points for longer periods of time. Don't get concerned about being so precise with the number of seconds you spend on each chakra that you get caught up in thought and become distracted from the real goal, doing the meditation. Desire and intention are emotional, not mental. Through regular practice you will get a comfortable sense of how long you are at each chakra. The keys are to keep the cycles short so you don't dwell for minutes at a time at each chakra, and to focus on your pure desires and intention.

Om Nama Shivaya Will Produce Miracles

This new century will be a very powerful time, and it is indeed the Age of Miracles. You will be elevated to a new reality. There will be miracles on a personal level and on a universal level. Recently I received an e-mail that carried three lines. The e-mailer said that he taught the One Minute Om Nama Shivaya Meditation to a lady who never meditated before. Here was the miracle. The lady went into a deep trance in response to the mantra Om Nama Shivaya. Use these tools and share them with others. Some of you may want to experiment with chanting OM NA MA SHI VA YA in groups on a weekly basis.

Chapter 8

The Karma-Busting Mantra

*Use Thiru Neela Kantam to erase
negative events from your life.*

When self-help people tell me that you create your own reality, I tell them this is only true in a limited sense. There have been many self-help books, but how many people have been able to turn around their life? They have been reading hundreds and hundreds of books on self-help which all say you create your own reality and the Universe is the limit. You are a totally unlimited being. Yet, how many of you have dramatically changed your life? What is the percentage of people who have been able to change their life? One percent? Two percent?

In fact, ninety-eight percent fail. This is what people have to look at. How many of us have been able to change our life although we all wanted to change our life not now, but five years ago?

For most people, significant manifestation has not happened yet. Day by day we wake up in the same old reality. We get frustrated. Even people who write books saying that you can do everything get frustrated, although they may not acknowledge it.

So there is a reality that is very difficult to change. These are the givens. And we created this reality. And that is what we need to diffuse.

The Diffusion of Karma Cannot Be Done by the Mind

The most important thing that you have to understand is that you cannot use your human mind to change your life. Mentally, you can go on making affirmations, writing affirmations, making promises that "I won't repeat this, I will change this, I won't repeat this behavior." But then you will find that you are in the same cloud, in the same place, in the same situation. Why is that? Because of karma. Karma is the spell. Everyone is under a spell. In Sanskrit they have a word called "samskara" which means innate qualities or certain proclivities with which you are born. That is the karma from a previous birth.

Change Your Life through the Use of Sound

The real way to dramatically change your life is through sound. Consciousness itself is sound. So if you change sounds within the system, you can make lasting changes in your life.

All that you need to do is to change the sounds of your consciousness at a very deep level. When the yogis talk about sounds, they don't talk about only the spoken sounds. Spoken sounds are only a very gross form of sounds. Spoken sounds emerge from unmanifest levels.

The Theory of Sounds

Sounds, fundamentally, are the building blocks of the whole Universe. Sounds build your body; sounds build your mind; sounds build everything that you see around you. Without sounds, nothing can exist. The seers of ancient India knew the secret of sounds and they gave them in formulas that can make significant changes in your life. By using these sounds, either in meditation or listening to mantras, you are creating a very powerful environment within your own consciousness. The sounds affect your mind in a profound way, enabling you to acquire a new mind.

Mantras Will Produce Dramatic Results

The evolution of speech is like this: first, there is sound, then a thought (thought also has a sound), then a pre-thought sound, then a "nada" (sound current of the subtle body), and then "paranada" (highest transcendent or Soundless Sound). In order to make significant changes in your life, all you need to do is rearrange the sound patterns of your own consciousness. That's what mantras do. Mantras are sounds of the unconscious. While using the mantra, the mantra takes you very deep into the layers of the unconscious. That's why people who use mantras get dramatic results.

Superficial Change versus Deep Change

If you try to change your consciousness at the mind level, the change will be very superficial because it cannot dispel the spell you are under. By clinging onto the mantra, you can go into a deeper level and rearrange the sound atoms of your own consciousness. In that way you can restructure your reality. Not only do you diffuse your karma, you also restructure it. There are mantras to bust your karma first and that helps to create more awareness. And then the restructuring process is done through other mantras, special sounds used for creation.

Bust Your Karma with the Mantra Thiru Neela Kantam

You can diffuse your karma, or "bust" your karma by using the karma-busting mantra Thiru Neela Kantam (pronounced Tee-Ru Nee-La Kan-Tam). This mantra is used to diffuse the subtle psychic vibrations of karma that reside in the throat. Every day when you arise in the morning, chant the mantra silently or out loud for three minutes. Do this every day and you will begin the process of changing your life for the better. If you have my karma-busting CD Sounds for Karma-Busting, you can play that during the day, in the background, or use it for your own meditation. By using the sound Thiru Neela Kantam, either in meditation or listening to the sounds in the chant, you will be creating a very powerful environment within your own consciousness.

The Story of the Karma-Busting Mantra

The sound Thiru Neela Kantam was given to mankind by Lord Shiva at the beginning of creation. A mythological story describes the event of the demons and the gods churning the ocean of milk to extract the elixir of immortality. A snake was used as a rope for churning. When the elixir was emitted, the snake also vomited poison, which fell on the elixir. Shiva, the great and most compassionate being, came forward and swallowed the poison. The poison remained in his throat. Myths are the language of the Divine, and convey eternal truths. The throat is the location for poison, or negative human consciousness.

Every time you speak or hear or meditate on the sounds of Thiru Neela Kantam and focus on your throat, you are immediately transported to the cosmic event when Shiva drank the poison. This helps to diffuse your karma. Thiru Neela Kantam is a magical sound. Use it every day to transform your life and change your destiny.

～

Chapter 9

Change Your Bad Money Karma

*Your past life karma stops you
from making money.*

Most people in the world have bad money karma, which means they are hurting for money. This is true even in the United States, which is the richest country in the world. Most people experience one or more of the following:

▲ Living from paycheck to paycheck.

▲ No paycheck at all.

▲ Living with their parents.

▲ Driving a junky car.

▲ Taking a bus to work because they don't have a car.

▲ Job is constantly ending and continually looking for another.

▲ Surviving on cash advance from credit cards.

▲ Borrowing money from others.

If you go to a financial counselor he or she would say one or more of the following:

▲ You have no job skills that are marketable.

▲ Go back to school and acquire some education.

▲ Get two full-time jobs to supplement your income.

▲ Get more hours wherever they are available.

I am not going to emphasize any of the aspects mentioned above. Not that I disbelieve them, but they are commonplace knowledge and many people, if not everyone, know about them. I want to give you some uncommon and spiritual methods for addressing your money karma.

Why You Don't Have Money

Why do you hurt for money? There are many reasons why you don't have money. Let me begin from the beginning of your life. Your mother has just delivered you. But, unfortunately, you are not born with a silver spoon. One's birth circumstances with money constraints have serious consequences. As a child growing into adulthood, you are not going to have an easy life unless your parents do something to improve their finances. But as the book, *Rich Dad, Poor Dad* indicates, most of our dads (including mine) had no clue as to how to make money.

In a negative parental environment like this, you can do very little to get up and running. Your consciousness is clouded and you have no energy. You can't go to a good school because you can't afford the tuition. Why is this happening to you and not to Prince William or the sons and daughters of a millionaire? There is only one answer to the question: You are born with bad money karma.

How You Can Change Your Money Karma

I have come to this earth plane primarily to help people change their karma. In order for you to have maximum results, you should follow my advice meticulously:

▲ Get rid of any negative philosophy about money. This has not helped you. Remember, even without your knowledge, your philosophy will sneak in. Get rid of it, period.

▲ Start my two-fold program to improve your bad money karma outlined below:

1. First, get rid of your past life karma that is disallowing you to make money. When you wake up in the morning, do the karma-busting mantra Thiru Neela Kantam at least for three minutes while still in bed. Mentally chant the mantra Thiru Neela Kantam in the throat, visualizing a blue light. Both the mantra and the light should stay in the throat. Make a prayer to me to empower the mantra for you to remove your bad money karma.

Later on when you shower, do the mantra again as out-lined. After a shower, take a few flower petals (or even a whole flower) and roll them on your head (around the brain area and forehead), throat, neck, shoulders and chest (heart area). As you do this, pass your bad money karma to the flower petals. Put the mantra Thiru Neela Kantam into each area. Let the negative thoughts about money in your head pass into the flower. Let the bad money karma stored in the throat pass into the flower. Let the financial burdens carried in the right shoul-der and left shoulder pass into the flower. Literally let the burden lift off your shoulders. Let any heartache and sorrow about money and finances in your heart pass into the flower.

Do not smell the flower petals. Hold them in your right hand as you do the ritual. Imagine that the flower petals have absorbed all your past-life karma and present-life karma and then crush them, saying the mantra Thiru Neela Kantam. Then throw these scapegoat flower petals away and wash your hands. There are many beautiful esoteric secrets regarding flowers, and I suggest some of these will open up for you if you work faithfully with this technique.

Tell yourself firmly, "I do not want to go through this karmic life. I must dissolve it and create some other karma, something more fruitful." If you do this flower ritual every day, your human ego and doubt will get out of your way. You will begin to desire in a more authentic way. What supports a prosperous mind are desires that are authentic, genuine and healthy. Without desires, a prosperous mind falls apart. So I repeat this truth to you, what supports prosperity is desire. So the fire of alert consciousness and desire must be burning all the time. You must cultivate that consciousness. When the mind begins to chatter, say "Shut up!" and put something interesting in the mind instead. If more and more people will live this teaching, we can create a society of conscious individ-uals.

I have created a special CD with the Thiru Neela Kantam mantra, and those of you who have the CD *Sounds for Karma-Busting* should listen to it every day.

2. Your money karma is carried out in life through the planets, through your personal astrology. I recommend that you find out which planets are directly involved in creating financial hardships for you and do some remedies to change those bad influences. You may ask, "If I am doing Thiru Neela Kantam, why bother with planets?" The answer to this question is: Thiru Neela Kantam is your general physician. He knows everything about your body, but he needs to send you to an eye doctor or an orthopedic doctor as the need arises.

Financial Analysis to Identify Your Malefic Planets

My ashram astrologers in India can do a financial analysis for you to identify the malefic (harmful) planets in your horoscope and make recommendations for remedies to alleviate their influence.

The Manifestation Mantra and Meditation

*The sound Ah has the ability
to attract everything to you.*

Thies chapter contains two techniques you can use for manifestation, the Ah meditation and the Ara Kara mantra. Both contain the powerful Ah sound. The sound Ah has the ability to attract whatever you strongly and clearly desire. The sound Ah is a key component of the Ara Kara manifestation mantra that has been kept secret for many centuries. Ara Kara is a resonance chord for prosperity, perfect health, and enlightenment.

Ara Kara Alters the Atomic Structure of Your Mind

Ara Kara is a supreme mantra capable of attracting desired outcomes into your life. The mantra Ara Kara is a powerful sound capable of altering the atomic structure of your mind. By understanding how these sounds can change your mind, you can learn to change your life by changing and regulating your mind. The sounds Ara Kara have the ability to attract everything to you. The sound AH is the embodiment of desire. RA symbolizes the fire energy, and KA is an important principle of materiality. The sounds Ara Kara can transform a psychological reality into a material reality. When you vibrate with the sounds Ara Kara, your thoughts also begin to vibrate with the sounds Ara Kara. This is the key. Your thoughts will now have the ability to manifest in a three-dimensional form.

Pittsburgh, Pennsylvania 1992

Sedona, Arizona 1995

Tamil Nadu, India 2000

Greenwich, Connecticut 2000

The Ah Meditation

The secret meditation for manifestation that I gave to Wayne Dyer and which he presented in his book *Manifest Your Destiny* is called the Ah Meditation. Time and again I hear stories of individuals manifesting cars, houses, jobs and other things they desire, using this meditation. Bring any thought that you want to manifest to the third eye and interject this thought with the sound Ah. This sound has the power to empower your thoughts. I gave this meditation to Wayne and told him, "Experiment with this in your life and if it works, take it to the world." Wayne did take it to the world and now at least a million people are using this technique.

The Sound of Creation

The basis for the Ah Meditation is that creation takes place in two centers. One is the sex center, the sex chakra (located by the reproductive organs), from which the energy is released to create a baby. Creating a baby is a mystery, a joyous act. You can also create through the third eye chakra, which is between the two eyebrows and the pituitary gland. Everyone has an option to create either through the sex chakra or through the third eye chakra. You create through the sex center to create a baby, but the same energy can be taken to the third eye chakra and can be released from there.

The New Ah Meditation

Since sharing the Ah Meditation with the world through Wayne Dyer, I have made some refinements to this meditation. You should meditate to the sound Ah, repeating it out loud and use it to raise your Kundalini energy (the energy of pure desire, a spiritual energy which lies dormant at the base of the spine in the sacrum bone) from the base of your spine to your third eye chakra. Then you should also speak out loud about the thing you are trying to manifest:

▲ I must, must, must have it!

▲ I must, must, must have it!

▲ I must, must, must have it!

(The word "must" is like a mantra. It must carry the emotions when you say it.)

▲ Not having it is not an option!

▲ Not having it is not an option!

▲ Not having it is not an option!

45

Make these statements with conviction and passion. Bring all the passion, all the senses together to see, hear and feel your manifestation. Embrace your manifestation. Hold on to your manifestation. Emotionalize the sound Ah. Mentally have the sound Ah pierce through the images of your manifestation. After your meditation, let go and allow God to manifest for you what you want. Do not worry about it. Do not analyze it. Hold on to the image and energize it with the sound Ah.

Negativity and Doubt Will Stop Manifestation

Negativity and doubt will stop the process of manifestation. The human mind itself is negative and that is why you must use will power to control your mind, to control your thoughts. God will find a million ways to help you. God will open many doors for you. Somebody will knock on your door with a new opportunity, right out of the blue. This is how the process of manifestation occurs. The way to stop the blessings from coming into your life is to disbelieve. You will get everything, not through your human ego, but through the grace and love of God. Do not forget this.

Chapter 11

Tools for Advanced Ritual and Practice

You can bring in powerful
spiritual energies with sacred tools.

Tthere are many spiritual tools available to enhance and accelerate your
spiritual progress. They will attract spiritual energy to you, focus your
attention, and even dissolve your karma. These tools have been used
in India for thousands of years.

Vibhuti (Sacred Ash)

Sacred ash (vibhuti) is to be used in meditation practice on your forehead
and optionally, on other parts of your body. The vibhuti I provide comes
from India, created under careful preparation according to my highest standards.

This is a tool that comes from the Divine to assist you in opening your
third eye and absorbing spiritual realization at an accelerated pace. In addition, sometimes spiritual seekers are not able to attract things because they
lack authentic desire. The sacred ash has properties for both erasing karma
and for helping you to develop authentic desire.

I recommend using the vibhuti after showering, before beginning a
meditation session. You may apply it using the right hand, using your ring
finger and dotting the third eye area on the forehead (traditionally, the use
of the index finger in applying vibhuti is reserved for one's teacher).

Or you can use the middle, ring and pinkie finger of the right hand to
create a three-stripe effect on your forehead or even liberally apply completely across your forehead as a protective blessing during these volatile

times, chanting OM NA MA SHI VA YA during the application.

I also suggest, in addition to the forehead, that you put some vibhuti on your throat and on your shoulders. If you wish, you may put the contents of the packets into a small enclosed glass box or other suitable container and keep the vibhuti near your meditation spot or altar. It is okay to wash off your face before leaving the house. Some people apply a very light amount all over their body before going to sleep at night.

Two Functionalities of the Sacred Ash

The sacred ash has two functions. It will dissolve your sins that block your progress and will give you the ability to desire deeply and without judgments. I call the sacred ash the desire powder. If you want to manifest, you need to learn how to desire. Don't get me wrong. Most human people do not know how to desire. Yes, all of you desire, but you desire without passion.

There is a story about the ash. Shiva opened his third eye and burnt down the god of desire (Manmatha). He then put the ash all over his body. Smearing the vibhuti on your body is a sacrament. When you regularly use the vibhuti you will develop ability to desire through the grace of Shiva.

Shiva-Shakti Mala Beads

Rosaries have traditionally been used in both the West and the Far East for spiritual devotions. In India, the rosary, which is called a mala, has been used as an important spiritual tool for thousands of years for counting recitations of mantras. Typically, malas come in a necklace form with either 108 or 54 beads (twice around a set of 54 beads equals a count of 108). The best mala beads are composed of both rudraksha beads and crystal beads. Rudraksha is a small berry that hardens and which is drilled and strung. It is found in many locations throughout the Far East, and varies in its spiritual quality.

Rudraksha beads, which symbolize Lord Shiva, increase the power of your mantras. Crystal beads, which symbolize the Goddess, store the spiritual power contained in the mantras. Lord Shiva gives spiritual evolution, and the Goddess gives material possessions. According to the sacred scriptures of India, the Universe is created when the masculine (Shiva) and feminine (Shakti) elements come together. The process of creation of matter occurs when the male energy is ignited by the female energy. When you use malas with both rudraksha and crystal, you are strengthening the balance between spirituality and materiality in your life. Using both these types of beads will give you the very best results in chanting mantras.

I have created my own custom-designed Shiva-Shakti malas using both rudraksha and crystal beads. Only rudraksha of the highest spiritual quality is used for these custom malas. Some people like to wear the mala beads to access this spiritual power stored in them.

A mala has one bead at the end that is called the "meru" (the Sanskrit word for "mountain"). This bead contains the accumulated spiritual energy of all the mantras recited using the mala. When using a mala, you should not "cross over" the meru. When you reach the meru, you should start counting backwards, until you reach the meru again, and then continue backwards again, never crossing over the meru.

Crystal Shiva Linga

A Shiva Linga is a powerful ritual and meditation tool. The linga is a symbolic icon representing the male and female generative organs. This is an ancient sacred, tantric symbol for the creative and powerful energies of the Divine. This is a potent form of Lord Shiva containing both the masculine and feminine energies of the Divine, the sum of Divine Intelligence and Compassion. Crystal is a material that amplifies subtle vibrations. It is used in meditative arts only for positive purposes. Doing ritual and meditation practice with a crystal Shiva Linga accelerates the practice.

Some people keep a crystal Shiva Linga on their meditation table or altar. I suggest that you make a daily practice of pouring a small amount of liquid over a crystal Shiva Linga. You can put the crystal Shiva Linga in a small cup, pour a small amount of milk or water or juice over the Shiva Linga, reciting the chant OM NA MA SHI VA YA a few times. This simple practice strongly focuses and energizes your prayers and brings Divine energies into your daily life.

When done, rinse off the crystal Shiva Linga and dry it off. Some people place a flower or offer incense or candlelight when they return the crystal Shiva Linga to their meditation table or altar. If you want to drink the liquid you poured over it when it was in the small cup, that is fine, as a kind of "communion."

Candles

In India, fire is the messenger between human beings and the gods. Fire is called Agni. Agni himself is a god. He creates gold out of mud and is pure energy. Lighting a candle brings in powerful spiritual energies and immediately transforms your space. I have never seen a ritual more powerful than lighting a candle. Lighting a candle brings different energies into focus. It creates the flow of Divine energy. Having one or more candles burning at your altar is a potent tool for drawing spiritual energy into your life.

An ancient practice for immortality and purification is to keep five candles burning when you go to sleep. The Siddhas taught if there is enough light, there won't be any disease. You must use common sense if you try this. Have smoke alarms and good ventilation and so forth, and only use candles that have lead-free wicks and are safe. Some people have found candles that can burn all night safely, the kind some churches use in their sanctuaries. If you cannot do five, that is okay. Do what you can. Even one candle burning at night is purifying. But again, only do this if you can do it safely. Some people with pets or small children will not be able to do this safely.

Flowers

Flowers contain energy from space. You can speak your prayers to the flowers and offer them to deities. You can energize your life by having a flower on your altar. Handling flower petals brings you in contact with a very pure vibration. You can use flowers to dissolve karma by rubbing flower petals on your body.

There is a gesture some people like to do to honor the sacred use of these flowers. When the flower petals have dried up, do not discard them in the trash. Flowers that have been used in spiritual offerings can be scattered onto the earth, someplace where people will not walk on them, and they will just recycle into the earth. Some people who live in city apartments with no yard, collect their used flower offerings into a paper or plastic bag and scatter them in a park or field when they take a walk in open nature.

Flowers come from a very pure dimension. They carry space energy, the energy of akash (space). Your karmic records are said to be stored in the Akashic Records, the realm of space energy. And flowers have the occult (hidden) power to help you access Akashic Records. This spiritual technology is like directly updating a database! I promise you, if you work with the flower petals and the karma-busting mantra Thiru Neela Kantam, you will find tremendous benefit.

The flower ritual comes from Divine law, not human law. Divine law deals with spirit. It is difficult to change deep-seated karma through behavioral techniques. This technique is part of Divine Knowledge, and many, many people in the world will now benefit from it. Repeat this flower ritual every day.

Yantras

Energized yantras are a meditation tool. They frequently contain a geometric form of some kind and other inscriptions, which contain a sort of "short cut" opening to various interdimensional planes of light associated with various deities.

The Siddha masters are adepts in the use of yantras to attract things towards them. Yantras are magical diagrams with squares, triangles, and circles in a certain permutation combination.

Each deity has its own magical yantra. The yantra is the conduit through which you connect with the deity. These magical diagrams were cognized by the Siddhas in deep states of samadhi. In Hindu temples in India, they bury the corresponding yantra of the god or goddess underneath the deity in order to energize the statue of the deity.

I will give you a specific example. There had been a money crunch in my computer company in New York. I ordered a custom-designed special yantra to attract money, business and people. I installed the yantra and within 24 hours, the company started attracting money. It was miraculous. Just before the money started coming, there was a big pandemonium in the company. This is how the yantras work. There are yantras for relationships, health and for cleaning up the energy of the office space or house, and for many other purposes.

I know that yantras work and I want to make sure that I put my energy intent into your yantras. It is very important for me to do that to make the yantra come alive with full power. We make many yantras available through my web site at *www.srisiva.com*. Keep in mind that the yantras we offer may vary from time to time.

Some examples of yantras that we make available:

▲ Ganesha Yantra (to remove obstacles)
▲ Dana Akarshana Yantra (to attract cash, business opportunities, prosperity, home, car)
▲ Muruga (Sadakshara) Yantra (to remove debts)

▲ Navagraha Yantra (to remove bad influences from the planets)
▲ Sudarshana Yantra (for protection from negative influences and for purifying)
▲ Shiva Yantra (for enlightenment and prosperity)

The way to use the yantra is to place it on an altar. You can bathe it with milk, orange juice and honey on full moon days. Other days, you can light a candle and incense and pray to it, just like you would pray to an image of a deity. You should offer a flower and a raisin or other fruits. Repeated prayers will make the yantra come alive. Some people like to do an eyes-open meditation focusing on a yantra and perhaps chanting a mantra associated with the deity associated with the yantra.

The yantras that I offer are very special. They contain inscriptions in Sanskrit associated with a specific deity. They have each been energized through a special ritual. Just having the yantra on your meditation table or altar will bring the benefit of that energy. Meditating with them will heighten the intensity of your meditations and prayers.

Spiritual Imagery

Meditating on sacred images is mythotherapy. These images directly affect the unconscious mind. Working with the unconscious opens up the realm of miracles, the realm of outrageous thinking. We need to change our realities. We don't want to wait; we want it now. The moment you make a decision that you want it now, you create the situation. It all starts with an inner decision.

Spiritual images are powerful tools for attracting spiritual energy. If you place my image on your altar, for example, I will send you spiritual energy for Prosperity and Enlightenment.

▲ **Shiva** – Lord of Infinite Intelligence and Compassion, the Doorway to Enlightenment, Removal of Karma
▲ **Lakshmi** – Goddess of Abundance, Beauty and Prosperity
▲ **Ganesha** – Lord of the Planets and Remover of Obstacles
▲ **Saraswati** – Goddess of Knowledge, Education and All Forms of Scientific and Creative Arts
▲ **Brahma** – Creative Energy
▲ **Vishnu** – Wealth, Enjoyment of the Material Plane

▲ **Parvati** – Wisdom of Yogic Discipline and Energy to Pursue Self-Discovery

▲ **Durga** – Destroyer of Negative Energies Preventing Joy

▲ **Krishna** – Triumphant Confidence and Giver of Victory, and

▲ **Kali** – Destroyer of Ignorance and Illusion

Money Imagery

To attract money, put up pictures representing financial abundance. Put up a picture of a money tree. The money tree goes back to the archetypal imagination of the human race. There ARE money trees in heaven. They are not just money trees, but these are trees that are capable of manifesting the things you want. They are called wish-fulfilling trees. In Sanskrit there is a name for such a tree. It is called Kalpa Vriksha, the trees that manifest your desires. So, it's important to visualize because the money tree belongs to the unconscious and the archetypal imagination.

Trident Visualization

Visualize the trident, a three-pronged weapon. This weapon will give you courage. Put pictures of a trident around you, and let the power of this symbol sink in deeply. We see the trident in many places as a symbol of great confidence. King Neptune has a trident; the U.S. Navy SEALS use the trident on their pin. Some of you may want to get pictures of Lord Shiva sitting with a trident. Meditating on this form as a mandala or yantra brings courage. For the positive energies of meditation to flow properly, you must have an attitude that is victorious, triumphant, and confident. You must bring up your courage, get your "yang" up, to fully engage in successful risk taking.

Focus on the Square

To help you make changes about material comfort, you should focus on the sacred geometry of the square. The four sides of a square represent the number four, and the four sides will help you to "square things away." Both the geometric shape of the square and the number four contain energies which complete material formation. Squares or rectangles give a solid foundation for material life.

Just by looking at squares, so many things will correct themselves. If you don't have a house, if you don't have a good body, if you don't have a good car, then something has gone wrong. What has gone wrong is that you have an amorphous consciousness. Your consciousness is not supporting any form. So, we are going to create a form here for you to focus on because form is clarity. Understand this: clarity and form are synonymous. You will get clarity just by looking at a square, which is a very structured form.

You must establish this square consciousness within yourself. Draw a square. Carry a square and put it on the refrigerator, on your books, on your table, wherever it will enable you to look at it frequently. By looking at the square, you are going to "square away" or put many things in your life in order. This is what sacred geometry is going to do for you.

❧

Written Goals

Focus your mind with written goals.

For manifestation to take place in your life, you must be very clear about your goals. That is why it is very important for you to write down not only long term goals but also goals for every single month of the year. In the popular motivational book, *Think and Grow Rich* by Napoleon Hill, he directs readers to write a "Definite Chief Aim" for your life. This "Definite Chief Aim" is to be read out loud every day when you get up in the morning and every night before you go to bed. This tool is powerful because it clarifies your goals and focuses your mind on your goals.

Having a great idea and making it a goal is an important step to changing your life; having the courage to make it real is what distinguishes reality from fantasy. If you haven't done so already, first create a grandiose fantasy for yourself. Think about how you would like your life to look in areas such as finances, relationships, health or service to society. Next, think about what steps you would be willing to take to help you realize that fantasy.

Now, take a reality check so you are properly prepared to make your fantasy come true. It's good to take a risk, provided it's a carefully thought out one that's calculated to bring you success. For example, before leaving a job to start a business, consider that business's true potential. Is there enough demand for this product or service, so that success is a reasonable possibility within a reasonable time frame? Do you have enough money set aside to survive for six months or a year while you build your business? How can you create the money needed to live and to start a new business?

Focus on Your Goals

Each month, you should set personal goals based on specific themes for your life. Repeat these goals out loud. Also, write out your goals by hand several times a day (nine is a good target number). Morning is best since it will help you consciously set your intended thoughts for the day. Writing a goal is a very powerful and moving ritual. Rituals will help to turn your positive thoughts and habits into second nature. Visualize the manifestation of these goals. Focus on these goals when you chant OM NA MA SHI VA YA. Always remember your goals.

Keep Track of Your Progress Every Month

You do not manifest because you do not remember what you want to manifest. Oppositional forces will try to knock down your goals. Keep your consciousness fully focused on your goals. Keep track of your progress every month. When you achieve one of your goals, write it down. Keep a record of your goals and the progress in achieving your goals. Your monthly personal goals are designed to build off one another, so it's important to regularly work with them (each day is ideal). For example, once you realize more money through your new ideas about personal finance, you have the foundation to make even more progress with the next goal, risk taking.

Personal Transformation Program

I offer a one year home study course Sri Siva's *Personal Transformation Program* that utilizes 12 videotapes and assignments from a monthly workbook to sharply focus your goals. The workbook contains a worksheet on which you write down your monthly goals, and which gives practical techniques to use the mantra of the month to empower your monthly goal. There are 12 areas of focus including:

Month 1—*Physical Appearance and Personality*
Enhance your physical, psychological and soul beauty.

Month 2—*Finances*
Acquire new forms of knowledge about finance and creating money.

Month 3—*Risk Taking*
Develop an extra-ordinary consciousness and courage.

Month 4—*Material Comforts*
Manifest the home and car of your dreams.

Month 5—*God*
Empower yourself with a personal connection with God.

Month 6—*Health, Enemies, Debts and Litigation*
Counteract principles of negativity.

Month 7—*Relationships*
Fulfill your desire for meaningful relationships.

Month 8—*Obstacles and Longevity*
Solve unforeseen difficulties, obstacles and obstructions of energy.

Month 9—*Compassion and Grace*
Seek compassion to earn the grace of God.

Month 10—*Profession*
Contemplate business opportunities that combine fulfillment and money.

Month 11—*Profit*
Assess the market for a business opportunity and ascertain the potential profit.

Month 12—*Enlightenment*
Reclaim your true nature and realize your unity with God.

Chapter 13

Develop the Positive Thinking Habit with the Thoughts and Rituals Scorecard

You become what you think.

A s the ancient seers have taught, you become what you think. So becoming conscious of the many different thoughts you have each day is a very important step in changing your life. You will be most effective in gaining control over your thoughts if you maintain a daily score-card of your thought experiences, which you will summarize at the end of each month. Make a copy of the scorecard in this chapter. Each day rate the intensity level of the positive and negative thought experiences you had on the scorecard below, using a scale of 1 through 10 (1 = weakest, 10 = strongest). At the end of the month summarize your daily scores for that month. Also check the amount of times each day that you performed the noted rituals and remembered the noted thoughts. These rituals are all discussed in this book.

It becomes quite interesting, and sometimes surprising, to learn just what holds your attention throughout each day and over extended periods of time. As you review your scorecards, you will begin to get a clearer picture of your thought patterns and your progress in changing those thoughts. Very soon, you will begin to see how these changing thoughts change your life.

To add a little extra momentum to your transformation process, identify a personal goal for yourself within the category you have identified for each month. Pick something that would have the greatest effect on every area of your life. For example, in my Personal Transformation Program, just listed in my previous chapter, month one focuses on personality and physical appearance. A personal goal might be to lose a certain amount of weight; exercise regularly; change something about the way you dress or look; notice whenever you are acting controlling with others, or are fearful, angry or jealous.

Once you've decided on your goal, write it down and then write it several times each day. Continue to examine yourself and see if you have the behaviors that you've identified. Rituals will help turn your positive thoughts and habits into second nature. Keep a daily scorecard of the number of times you remember to do the rituals listed on the next page. ☛

Scorecard

1. Positivity Scorecard: (Rate 1 – 10)

_____ Enthusiastic

_____ Optimistic

_____ Loving

_____ Patient

_____ Sharing

_____ Monthly personal goal

2. Negativity Scorecard: (Rate 1 – 10)

_____ Lethargy

_____ Negativity (e.g., fear, doubt, anxiety)

_____ Lack of focus

_____ Unconscious (not being fully alert and aware)

3. Rituals Scorecard: (Check the amount)

Wrote monthly personal goal
__ 0 – 10 times   __ 11 – 20 times   __ 21 – 30 times
__ 31 – 40 times   __ 41+ times

Applied sacred powder (vibhuti)
___ 0 times   ___ 1 time   ___ 2 times

Poured milk over a Shiva Linga
___ 0 times   ___ 1 time   ___ 2 times

Remembered "Om Nama Shivaya"
__ 0 – 10 times   __ 11 – 20 times   __ 21 – 30 times
__ 31 – 40 times   __ 41+ times

Remembered Sri Siva and gave thanks for his help
__ 0 – 10 times   __ 11 – 20 times   __ 21 – 30 times
__ 31 – 40 times   __ 41+ times

Chapter 14

Numbers to Change Your Destiny

*Meditating on certain numbers
can change your destiny.*

Recently I was watching television and saw on CNN that one Erika Greene was a winner in a multi-million dollar lottery drawing that took place. It reiterates several things that I have taught about karma, grace and numbers. There are many secrets about the use of numbers, and the visualization of specific numbers in certain patterns can alter your destiny.

I know of an Indian woman who was struggling pretty badly financially. But she had tremendous faith in Venkateswara, the Indian god of wealth (also known as Vishnu), and she trusted that one day he would help her to make a lot of money. She had a dream one night. The god appeared to her and showed her the winning numbers of a lotto and asked her to play that day. She asked her husband who was going to the grocery store to get her a ticket with the numbers she had seen in the dream.

However, she never told her husband about the dream and how she got those numbers. The husband came home, but he had forgotten to play the lotto. That night the prize was announced. The winning numbers were the same ones she saw in her dream. She ended up divorcing the guy.

The way that numbers can change your life is amazing. Use the special number grid included in this chapter. It contains nine numbers and they correspond to the nine planets in Vedic astrology. To bring positive change into your life, put these numbers in your consciousness. Inscribe the numbers on a thin copper plate. You can get a copper plate as thin as paper from a local craft or hobby store. Put it on your meditation altar. Repeat each number nine times, both horizontally and vertically, with your eyes closed. Offer candlelight, incense, flowers and some raisins. Pray to the numbers.

27	20	25
22	24	26
23	28	21

Chapter 15

Divine Grace through Nadi Astrology

*There may be records for your life written
in mysterious ancient palm leaves.*

This chapter may not appeal to everyone, but there are some people for whom this information will be a God-send. Literally. There are some people who are seeking a deeper explanation about their karma, what they did in a past life that has caused what they are dealing with now. So consider, have you ever wished for answers about why some things in your life look the way they do and what you could do to remedy some of your difficulties?

In India, there is a secret esoteric tradition that has kept records detailing the past, present and future for many people. This is called Nadi astrology. These records were written by various enlightened masters who are collectively called the Siddhas. I have mentioned them earlier in this book.

If you have been drawn to this book and have been finding it helpful, these enlightened Siddhas may have known you in a past life when you lived in India. If so, at that time they agreed to help you during a crisis in a future lifetime, and they always keep their word. For many people, that "future" lifetime is actually the one they are in now. The promised help they will receive will come from Nadi astrology.

If you are drawn to investigate Nadi astrology in this lifetime, there is a strong chance that you have a connection with these Siddhas and there are records waiting for you, sort of "Post-its" from the Divine, giving explanations and directions for this lifetime. Many traditions have predicted that this new millennium will be the setting for tremendous material and spiritual evolution for many people. Nadi astrology is a key tool for positive, rapid transformation as it explains past errors that have resulted in the current state of affairs in one's life and particular remedies to perform in order to alleviate difficulties and open up a new, more positive karmic track in this lifetime. I am very excited to share knowledge of this most precious tool and make it easily available to people in the West. The Nadis truly come from "the other side."

Siddhas and the Sacred Leaves

Many of the Siddhas are not yet well-known in the West, although one of them, Babaji, has been written about in Yogananda's book, *Autobiography of a Yogi*. Another book describing the yogic abilities of these masters is *Babaji and the 18 Siddha Kriya Yoga Tradition* by M. Govindan. In this millennium, the wisdom and secrets of the Siddhas are being passed into the West more openly for the first time, and I have special permission to share things which have never before been released publicly. Many people in the West will benefit enormously from them.

The enlightened Siddha masters founded Nadi astrology a long, long time ago. Lord Shiva, pleased with their devotion, bestowed upon them some exclusive powers. He gave them incredible clairvoyance to know the past, present and future. The Siddhas etched their priceless knowledge on ancient palm leaves called Nadis. Associated with you in your Poorva Janma (previous birth), they promised to help you in a future life, i.e., now. By the Nadi law, you will be involuntarily attracted to the leaves by destiny only. The very fact that you are reading this far into the description of the Nadis is an interesting omen, as not everyone even hears about them, let alone is curious about them.

The Nadi leaves were originally inscribed in Sanskrit. Various people have held the Nadis in secret once the Siddhas wrote them. One ruler, the Maharajah Serfoji II of Tanjore in southern India, was a true patron of art and science. He stored these palm leaves safely in his palace library knowing their importance. He also had them translated into Tamil (a language used in southern India). The British acquired possession of these leaves during their rule and later sold them to some families, which still own them and respectfully keep them. The Nadi leaves have been held quietly for centuries, waiting their time of rendezvous with their intended recipients, the individuals whose destinies they describe.

Time to Release Secrets

The time has come to release many of the Siddha secrets into the West in a broad way, to benefit many, many people. The time has come for this knowledge to go out to the masses. I have spent over twenty years of painstaking research in this life to unearth a combination of Nadis renowned for being genuine, accurate and reliable.

Most importantly for you, I am energetically involved in the remedial process of Nadi astrology which gives a very strong boost to the removal of negative karma and accelerates positive transformations. As suggested by Lord Shiva in your leaves, it is important to perform remedial rituals at specific temples, which hold ancient Divine energies. It is important for individuals to perform the remedies in order to change the problems in their lives, transmuting difficult karma created in past lives which may be affecting this one.

Finding Your Leaf, Changing Your Life

It is not enough to know your destiny, whether it is good or bad. An important step in creating a new life is the ability to change and reconstruct it as you wish it to be. This is a yogic art.

To find out if you have a leaf, your thumbprint is used as part of the "look-up" process. Everyone's thumbprint is unique. Nadi astrologers search through the palm leaves based on the pattern of the thumbprint to find out if you have a Nadi leaf containing your destiny, and remedial suggestions about how to remove negative karma. Nadi readings will accelerate the process of burning your karma and can completely alter the course of your destiny.

Some of the Nadi remedies may suggest that you visit a specific temple. These temples have been built in a sacred place with beneficial space. I also offer a service through my ashram where we can visit the temple for you, and by proxy, perform prescribed rituals to burn your karma.

Good Vibes and Bad Vibes

The Siddhas considered water a great purifier. Space itself also has therapeutic properties when it is the right space. According to the Siddhas, each space has its own vibes. This can be clearly understood by a comparison of a "good" neighborhood and a "bad" neighborhood. The Siddhas tell a story to explain the vibes in different geographical spaces.

Story of the House of Thieves

Once a Siddha was caught in rain in the woods. It was dark at night, and he looked around for a shelter. He found a house and walked towards it to sit out the rain, as the house was covered. He also found a newly wedded couple taking shelter. The Siddha had a terrible thought suddenly flashing through his mind. That was to kill the husband and take the woman and her jewels. The Siddha examined how this negative idea came to him. He discovered that the house belonged to some robbers, and their thought waves were still floating in the sky, and the Siddha happened to access them. Just as there are negative thought patterns floating in the atmosphere, there are also good ones. The places where good thoughts are floating are called sacred spaces. Usually these are within specially built temples where in ancient times a great being cured the king of a disease or healed the poor, and so forth. To visit a sacred space and to breathe the vibes there is truly therapeutic.

Good Thoughts and Sacred Spaces

So the temples recommended by the Nadis are dripping with space energy from the Siddhas. This is why remedies and prayers performed in them are so effective. There is Infinite Intelligence and Compassion present in the Divine radiations of these temples. Each temple is devoted to an aspect of the Divine. Those that are given as your "remedy" temples are keyed to energies suitable for diffusing your old karma and recharging you with a new life. A temple called Vaitheeswaran Koil in a village in southern India is the nerve center of the Nadi tradition. Surrounded by other temples of great significance, the entire village reverberates with this ancient heritage of wisdom. The Nadi readers I work with are from this fertile Nadi astrology soil; I guarantee the authenticity and integrity of the readers and Nadis used by Vaaak Sounds.

Caution! There is so much out there in the name of Nadi astrology—not every Nadi is comprehensive or legitimate. It is important to be cautious about the source.

Two Ways to Find Your Nadi Leaf

For those who are interested in exploring this sacred tool, you can find your Nadi leaf through two means: by coming to India in person (either on one of the Vaaak Sounds special group trips or on an individually-designed trip for those of you with tight and unpredictable schedules); or through use of an efficient mail-order service.

In the case of using the mail-order service, my staff in India will arrange for remedies to be performed in your Nadi temples in your name, and this has great efficacy. You may be given a yantra to use at home, and in that case, you must be faithful to this for the remedy to work.

However, I have to be honest and say it is most beneficial to come to India and personally perform the remedies that the Nadi author prescribes for you. You are the best one to clean up your own mess! If you cannot travel to India at this point in time, you can receive your Nadi reading through the postal service or through e-mail. You may fill out a questionnaire and return it to Vaaak Sounds along with your thumbprint.

Some people start the process by opting for Nadi remedies through mail-order and then later come to India to repeat the remedies through the Nadi trip service. My ashram staff in India has been taking excellent care of people doing their Nadi remedies for several years now, and they really devote themselves to making this a deeply meaningful pilgrimage for you with the details of meals, hotels, transportation all attended to. You are accompanied by a Nadi guide who is familiar with the energies of the temples and who will ensure your remedies are properly performed. I have seen this to be a life transforming experience for many people, and I know there are many, many more leaves waiting for their rightful recipient.

Some people ask, "Some day can temples with special space energy be built in places other than India?" And I say, "Yes." We live in an age when new temples will be built in new lands, and when the Divine energies will charge new places as well. The time has come for enlightened energy to become available throughout the world. It is time for the Age of Miracles to take hold.

Nadi Reading Process

When you order your personal reading, Nadi readers will locate your leaf and any accompanying "chapters" of information. Then, the readers will locate your first chapter for a general reading. This information identifies you, your parents and spouse by name, number of siblings, profession, religion, and so on. It will include general predictions for your future.

The Nadi readers will then locate your two remedial chapters that prescribe the exact rituals to be performed, which can erase the balance of your past-life sins, allow you to end the current suffering and achieve your highest potential in the future.

Subsequently, you can request additional chapter readings on specific areas of life that you wish to learn about such as jobs, business, family, marriage, relationships, health/medical issues, and so on. But I insist that the most efficient way to start is with the remedial chapters. You have so much to gain by cleaning up the old karma!

There are many, many leaves waiting for souls that were meant to find them. This is a profoundly deep yogic science, and you cannot come to your Nadi before the time of the intended rendezvous. For some of you reading this book, that time is now.

Chapter 16

Astrological and Other Remedies

There are remedies that can change your destiny.

Astrology has enjoyed much popularity in the West for many years. The 6,000-year-old Hindu astrology system differs from Western astrology in several key areas. Whereas Western astrology focuses on personality and character analysis, Hindu or Vedic astrology (also called Jyotish) focuses on life circumstances and on events that are destined to occur in your life. Hindu astrology is based upon the philosophy of karma, with the premise that your current life is the result of actions you have had in previous births. Hindu astrology readings also differ from Western astrology in that they include recommendations for remedies to alleviate or mitigate karmic circumstances and events. These remedies include the prescription of specific gemstones to be worn touching your body, special mantras or rituals such as homas, also called pujas/poojas or yagnas/yagyas/yajnas.

Astrological Solutions

There are many excellent Hindu astrologers in India and now in the West as well. We also provide astrological counseling services and have the resources to fulfill the remedies as recommended in your astrological reading. One of the most important reasons you may not be succeeding in life can be found in the planets. I am convinced that every moment of your life is conditioned by the planets. A Vedic astrology reading, along with prescribed remedies, can do much to change your life for the better.

Homas

Homas are fire rituals that have been performed since ancient times to rain prosperity on individuals and humanity. Through my Nadi and Homa Center in Chennai, India, these rituals can be performed for you in India by deeply devotional Vedic scholars.

During the Vedic period in India (3,000 BC to 1,500 BC), the sages (seers) invoked the Divine beings to come to the earth through the use of homas. It is enlightening to know that the gods look to us as much as we look to them. Homas are thus the most ancient, yet one of the most effective and scientific approaches, to remove or reduce the pain and suffering we are undergoing due to our past sins.

There are specific homas not only used as remedies for problems found in your horoscope, but also homas to bring you wealth, health, improved relationships and success in life. The Lakshmi Kubera Homa is designed to bring immense wealth, the Navagraha Homa is a ritual for the nine planets that will eradicate karma, and there are other homas that can be performed at our Homa Center. I have personally developed the homas and they are performed by my staff with great care and sincerity.

Why Fire Rituals or Agni?

Fire converts mere sand into gold. It transforms hard rock into diamond. In this world, everything functions only with the aid of fire. We cannot cook our food without fire; neither can we digest the food that we eat. So a lot of homas performed in the Rig-Veda (one of the four major Vedas of Hinduism) were addressed to the Fire God. Our Rishis or Saints fully understood the powers of fire, one of nature's blessed elements.

Mail-Order Homas

For those of you residing in other parts of the world besides India, you can derive the benefits of homa without travelling to India. Through our unique mail-order plan, you can sponsor a homa specially tailored to your current life situation and future desires. My staff will perform the homa in your name with the utmost dedication, and then we will mail you some of the remnants of the precious items (known as "prasad") that were offered to the Fire God . These objects hold the blessings and concentrated energy of the deities invoked in the fire. You can use these objects in your meditation and prayer time to fulfill your desires. This is a great ancient science from holy India. Having these homas will help you gain in all walks of life.

Navagraha Trips

We offer special tours for groups and individuals to visit the principal temples of the nine planets, which are some of the greatest power spots in India (all located in and around Tamil Nadu). The experience of visiting these temples, which are very sacred places containing magical powerful energies, can be life transforming.

About Sri Siva

Sri Siva is a spiritual name given to Dr. Baskaran Pillai. (In past years, he has also been called Brzee, Sri Guruji and Guruji). Sri Siva is associated with an illustrious and esoteric lineage of enlightened Indian saints, the Tamil Siddhas, who have been passing on enlightened teachings for thousands of years, usually in very small circles of selected students.

Sri Siva was born in southern India and lived on the island of Rameswaram the first 18 years of his life. His spiritual journey started at an early age when he was given the opportunity to study and perform intensive meditation under the guidance of various eminent meditation teachers. He studied in numerous places, including the Himalayas. He received a very thorough initiation into the teachings of the Tamil Siddhas.

Concurrent with his mystic practices, he continued with his education in the university system and became a Research Fellow at the University of Madurai, India. His formal academic training in India resulted in a Master's Degree in English Literature and a Master of Letters in Comparative Literature from the University of Madurai, India. In 1983, he went to America and began graduate level studies concluding in a PhD in Religious Studies from the University of Pittsburgh.

He served as coordinator of Indian Studies within the Asian Studies Program at the University of Pittsburgh and taught several courses on Buddhist meditation and other Buddhist topics. His specialty was research on religious phenomena in light of modern science. He has training in neuropsychology, which he used in research to interpret traditional yogic and tantric wisdoms about psychobiology. He also served as an editor for the Encyclopedia of Hinduism.

Sri Siva is the first Tamil Siddha to travel to the West. He has permission to reveal secretive techniques of the Tamil Siddha enlightenment lineage to the world, techniques which have been kept secret since ancient times. Sri Siva has been teaching meditation for two decades and has taught seminars on successful thinking all over the world. He inspired noted author Wayne Dyer to write his best-selling book *Manifest Your Destiny*, which Wayne Dyer dedicated to him as "Guruji."

Sri Siva has been also actively involved in a study of Siddha Ayurveda herbs for healing purposes for the past two decades. He has sponsored several conferences of scientists in Siddha medicine. He is managing the development of a web site that will make available online numerous herbs from all over the world. He is leading efforts in research on the subject of herbs, and this information will become available in the future on his web site.

Sri Siva has privately consulted many leading industrialists and entrepreneurs in their business development and leadership skills over the years. He is currently heading several real-world business projects and is a very hands-on, practical businessman in the computer field with an office in the Silicon Alley section of Manhattan.

Sri Siva has presented at numerous conferences and shared panels at many universities with Nobel Prize laureates, including Eugene Wigner of Princeton University. He was invited by the United Nations World Religions conference as a speaker on Hinduism.

Sri Siva has also created the Tripura Foundation, a non-profit organization, through which he has done extensive good-will charity work. Sri Siva created the Tripura Foundation with the intention of eliminating hunger from the face of the world. A large portion of the profits from his various ventures goes toward supporting the Hunger Project.

Spiritually, he has been tasked with sharing in the West the mysteries of several ancient esoteric sciences including Nadi astrology and homas (fire rituals). The Tamil Siddha tradition, through Nadi astrology, has identified Sri Siva as a reincarnation of four great saints from ancient India:

▲ Agastya, the foremost Siddha and author of the Tamil language, as well as countless texts on astrology, alchemy, mantras, sastras, and medicine;

▲ Bhismacharya, a well-respected teacher of martial arts during the period of the epic *Mahabharata;*

▲ Manikavacakar, an illustrious Tamil saint who wrote several master-pieces of devotional lyrics on Lord Shiva, before dissolving into light; and

▲ Swami Ramalingam (Vallalar), an enlightened Indian saint in southern India who was graced with a light body and continued teaching until 1874, when he dissolved completely into light.

Agastya was a teacher of Babaji, whose lineage through Lahiri Mahasaya and Sri Yukteswar led to Paramahansa Yogananda. Yogananda was an enlightened teacher who came from India to America to teach in the 20th century and whose book, *Autobiography of a Yogi,* has been a perennial best-seller.

More stories about Agastya and Swami Ramalingam can be found in a more recent book, *Babaji and the 18 Siddha Kriya Yoga Tradition* by M. Govindan (see chapters 7 and 9).

Sri Siva wishes to give people both spiritual blessings and practical tools for self-improvement to accelerate their own material progress and path to spiritual enlightenment. He has widely toured to give public talks in many places throughout the world. Audiences experience a deep stillness as Sri Siva transmits pure Light with an energy that goes beyond words. At the same time, audiences also enjoy his ability to tell captivating stories with an excellent sense of humor.

About the Prosperity and Enlightenment Program

Pathway to Prosperity and Enlightenment.

Sri Siva is offering a special Internet-based Prosperity and Enlightenment program so busy people can receive teachings and blessing directly from him. This program allows him to create a personal connection, no matter where you or he might be at any given time. This program is for those of you who are interested in bringing more Light and abundance into your lives—whether that means more and better health, wealth, relationships, happiness or peace of mind; or perhaps a special and more personal dream. The structure, teachings and techniques will vary throughout the course of the program, based on what Sri Siva sees as the evolving needs of the group. You can visit the web site *www.srisiva.com* to access more details of this program.

～

The Tripura Foundation

*The easiest way to access God's grace is to
feed a famished human being starving for food.*

The easiest way to access God's grace is to feed a famished human being starving for food. Every day three billion people, nearly half of the population of the world, go to bed hungry. To address this situation, Sri Siva has created a 501(c)(3) tax-exempt non-profit organization, the Tripura Foundation, dedicated to abolishing world hunger and empowering the needy to reach a higher standard of life. A large portion of the profits from Sri Siva's various ventures goes toward supporting the Tripura Foundation.

The Tripura Foundation provides the basic necessities such as food, clothing and shelter to those in need. Striving to run a highly efficient organization, eighty percent or more of all funds collected goes directly to those in need.

Starvation is one hundred percent curable and poverty is one hundred percent reversible. In India, it takes only 22 cents U.S. to provide a meal for a hungry child. This comes to only $20 U.S. to feed a child for an entire month. Every penny counts. And, taking action to help feed the hungry is a powerful way to destroy the three demons of ego, maya, and karma. The Tripura Foundation charity projects are a pragmatic way to benefit the suffering of humanity and accelerate the process of attaining higher consciousness. It is Sri Siva's desire to see these charitable efforts grow and flourish and improve the quality of life for many, many people.

For more information...

...about Sri Siva's teaching programs and public events, meditation products, astrology and homa services, and charitable works, please visit the following Internet web sites:

> *www.srisiva.com*
> *www.tripurafoundation.org*

The *Products and Meditation Aids* section (following the Glossary), lists products that were mentioned earlier in the book. These products and more can be ordered online at *www.srisiva.com* or by sending payment to the following address. Please note that shipping is extra. If you are not ordering online, you should contact us before sending payment. Prices and availability are subject to change.

Vaaak Sounds
432 Allegheny River Boulevard, Suite 201
Oakmont, Pennsylvania 15139
Toll free:(888) 241-7337

Glossary

Age of Miracles - According to Sri Siva, a New Age that began on June 14, 2002. The prophesized "End of Times" in which God will come to the earth plane and bring a "Heaven on Earth." Also called Age of Truth, Age of Magic, and the Golden Age.

Ashram - Holy sanctuary. Teaching center. A spiritual place for spiritual instruction and/or spiritual practices.

Ayurveda - Ancient Hindu art of medicine and prolonging of life.

Avatar - An incarnation of God in human form.

Chakra - An energy center located in the body. A nerve center of the subtle body.

Goddess - Female representation or manifestation of Divinity.

Guru - Spiritual teacher.

Homas - Fire rituals that have been performed in India since ancient times to rain prosperity on individuals and humanity. Also called pujas/poojas or yagnas/yagyas/yajnas.

Kali Yuga - An age of time lasting 432,000 years. The Dark Age or Iron Age.

Kalki Avatar - Tenth avatar of Vishnu.

Karma - Action. Action not only as an impulse on the physical level, but also an impulse at a subtle or psychological level. Hence, thinking is action. Also known as the law of cause and effect.

Kundalini - Kundalini is the energy of pure desire, a spiritual energy that lies dormant at the base of the spine in the sacrum bone. This primordial cosmic energy lies coiled like a serpent and eventually, through the practice of yoga, rises up and awakens each successive chakra.

Lord Brahma - Form of the Hindu trinity. A deity governing creation.

Lord Shiva - Form of the Hindu trinity. A deity governing dissolution and re-creation of the Universe.

Lord Vishnu - Form of the Hindu trinity. A deity governing preservation.

Mala - A circle of stringed beads of various substances used in meditation.

Mantra - Spiritual or empowered speech. A short sacred text or prayer, often recited repetitiously.

Maya - The illusion of reality.

Meditation - To think deeply.

Nada - The sound current of the subtle body.

Nadi - A nerve fiber or energy channel of the subtle (inner) body. Nadis interconnect the chakras.

Nadi Leaves - Ancient sacred palm leaves which detail the past, present and future for many people.

Om - The mantra of the Divine.

Paranada - The first vibration from which creation emanates.

Parvati - A Goddess. The consort of Lord Shiva.

Prasad - Remnants of blessed ritual items.

Pujas/Poojas - See homas.

Samadhi - A transcendent state of consciousness. Absorption or bliss.

Samsara - The phenonmenal world where the soul's passage through a series of lives occurs.

Samskara - Innate qualities or certain proclivities with which a person is born. Karma from a previous birth.

Sanskrit - Vedic and mantric language. The oldest Indo-Aryan language.

Shiva Linga - A ritual and meditation tool to erase karma and receive blessings.

Siddha - A person with miraculous and magical power.

Sri - An Indian title of respect used for men. The title Shrimati is used for women.

Tamil Nadu - A state in southern India. The capitol is Chennai, formerly known as Madras.

Tantra - Esoteric Hindu rituals, disciplines and meditations.

Trident - A three-pronged weapon.

Vedas - The ancient sacred scriptures of India, of which there are four.

Vibhuti - A sacred ash that is used in meditation to erase karma and help attract material desires.

Yagna/Yagya/Yajna - See homas.

Yantra - A geometrical magical diagram used as a meditation tool with squares, triangles and circles in a certain permutation combination.

Yoga - Communion; union of the soul with the Divine, or a process which promotes that relationship.

Yogi - A person who practices yoga. The word **yogini** is the feminine form of the word.

Yuga - World ages. An age or extended period of time, of which there are four defined in Hinduism.

Products and Meditation Aids

Above 3 CD's for $40 when purchased as a set.

Myths are the language of the Divine, and convey eternal truths.

KARMA-BUSTING CD: The sounds Thiru Neela Kantam have the ability to dissolve karma. A mythological story describes the event of demons and the gods churning the ocean of milk to extract the elixir of immortality. $15.00

SOUNDS FOR MANIFESTING CD: The sounds Ara Kara have the ability to attract everything to you. The sounds Ara Kara can transform a psychological reality into a material reality. $15.00

MEDITATIONS AND AFFIRMATIONS WITH A MASTER CD: Morning Meditation, Chaotic Breathing, "Ham Sa" Breathing, Looking Up, "Ah" Meditation. Evening Meditation, Yogic Sleep, Daily Affirmations. $15.00

SHARABA CD (DESTROYING NEGATIVITY): For the first time, Sri Siva is making the *Sharaba* CD available to the general public. Previously this CD version of the mantra invoking the demon-destroying aspect of Lord Siva has only been sold to small numbers of students. $15.00

NEW! DANCING WITH SIVA CD: Sri Siva has gone into a professional recording studio to record the timeless mantras with modern music tracks. Sample the sounds online and preorder your copies! These make great gifts for friends or family. $15.00

SACRED ASH (VIBHUTI): Sacred ash (vibhuti) is used in meditation practice on one's forehead and optionally, other parts of one's body. This vibhuti comes from India, created under careful preparation according to Sri Siva's standards. In addition, sacred ash has properties for both erasing karma and for helping you with authentic desire.   Set of 4 pkts /$10.00

SHIVA-SHAKTI MALA BEADS: Mala beads are a special rosary used for counting recitations of mantras. Rudraksha beads are symbolic of Lord Shiva, and crystal beads are symbolic of the Goddess. Lord Shiva gives spiritual evolution, and the Goddess gives material possessions. Sri Siva has custom-designed these mala beads to give you the very best results in chanting mantras.   Set of 54 beads/$25.00

CRYSTAL SHIVA LINGA: A Shiva Linga is a powerful ritual/meditation tool, is a symbolic icon representing the male and female generative organs—the creative and powerful energies of the Divine: Divine Intelligence and Compassion. Crystal is a material which amplifies subtle vibrations. It is used in meditative arts only for positive purposes. $15.00

HINDU GODS AND GODDESSES by Swami Harshananda: This is a paperback book written in English and published by Sri Ramakrishna Math in India. It contains numerous interesting, easy-to-read stories about various aspects of the divine as described in the Hindu tradition. It has a wealth of information about the major Hindu gods and goddesses as well as information about the nine planetary beings and many of the minor deities who do not always get mentioned in other books. Generous black and white illustrations showing traditional artistic representations of these beings, plus useful index.   Book/$8.00

DEITY CARDS: High quality 5" x 5" cards suitable for framing. Set includes **Shiva** (Infinite Intelligence and Compassion, the Doorway to Enlightenment, Remover of Karma), **Lakshmi** (Purity, Beauty and Prosperity), **Ganesha** (Lord of the Planets and Remover of Obstacles) and **Saraswati** (Knowledge, Education and the Scientific and Creative Arts).   Set of 4/$8.00

PERSONAL TRANSFORMATION PROGRAM
VIDEO SERIES: Sri Siva has created a comprehensive program to empower individuals to
systematically transform every aspect of their
lives. Based on his personal experience of
guiding countless people to miraculous manifestations, this videotape and home study
course contains his most potent secrets for
transformation.

PTP Video Series (set of 12)/
$199.00

NEW! SRI SIVA SAMADHI WEEK
RETREAT VIDEOS: (Asilomar Retreat Dec.
24, 2001 - Jan. 1, 2002)—Give yourself a
rare, thorough glimpse into the true nature
of the Universe and yourself. According to
Sri Siva, many people are now ready to
receive teachings that were traditionally
taught only to small, select groups of
monks and serious students of
Enlightenment. Through a nine-day
journey, and 14 VHS videos, Sri Siva
provides clear, practical explanations of
powerful spiritual and material creation
concepts, sacred mantras and visualization
techniques, and direct experiences of
different levels of Samadhi. Each video is
90 min. long. (PAL format is available as a
special order. Contact us for more
information.)

Samadhi Week Videos (set of 14)/
$250.00

These products and more may be ordered
by contacting:

Vaaak Sounds
432 Allegheny River Boulevard, Suite 201
Oakmont, Pennsylvania 15139
Toll free: (888) 241-7337 or
fax: 412-828-0911

Purchase online at
www.srisiva.com